the story of PAT
****

NEWMAN PRESS • Paramus, N. J. / New York, N. Y. / Toronto / London

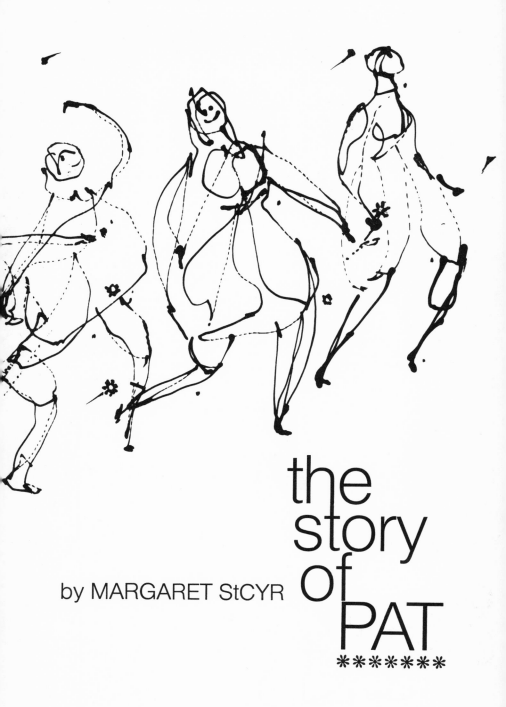

the
story
of
PAT
****

by MARGARET StCYR

To ARTHUR

"*H*as anything seemed strange to you over the last few months?" the specialist asked. "We'd like you to describe anything that seemed different from your first pregnancy."

The faces above me were grave: my own doctor, the specialist, a young interne. They examined my abdomen and took the baby's heartbeat. One question followed another. My abdomen had darkened ominously. "Be accurate," I told myself in spite of my fear. Our first child, Gail, had been delivered normally, easily. This time there was an abnormal heaviness—not like pregnancy weight—heaviness which left only at the onset of tonight's hemorrhaging. I no longer suffered the excruciating pain that had accompanied that unbearable weight.

"I haven't felt well or strong since my third month," I said.

My doctor nodded, pulling the sheet and blanket up to my shoulders. "See now if you can sleep a little for us tonight," he said. "You need the rest." (He was telling *me?*) "We'll do our very best by you and the baby."

The doctors exchanged a few long medical terms without looking at me again, then slowly took leave in sober silence.

Throughout the night nurses were kept busy with me. The hemorrhaging didn't subside. In an effort to arrest it, logs had been placed under the foot of my bed. I felt very weak, drowsy. I dozed fitfully.

Three years ago Arthur had driven me to this same hospital at a few minutes before midnight. I awoke the next morning to hear the nurse chant in my ear, "We have a lovely daughter for you, Mrs. StCyr. Seven pounds, two-and-one-half ounces." Sleepily I argued that she was dialing the wrong mother; mine was a boy. Accustomed to such responses from new mothers, she whispered, "Well, we'll wait until you are not so sleepy."

The nurse was right. We named her Gail Frances and for her first year she wore blue.

Only seven days ago, at dawn, my husband cautiously repeated the drive as I sat beside him praying for our second baby's chance of survival. The baby wasn't due for six weeks. I waited in a four-bed ward, grateful to hear Arthur describe the antics of our spirited blond daughter who waited at her grandmother's house for my return with her new playmate. It was mid-May; she would be searching for a new place to run with her wagon as the flowers were beginning to push their way through the earth she had trampled.

As the nurse brought in babies to the other three mothers, I continued to ask God that she would be doing the same for me in due time. My husband shared my forebodings and sent me a bouquet of pink sweet peas and baby's breath. I felt reassured dwelling on another handful of sweet peas arranged in a corsage, the gift of my good-looking, dark-haired senior prom escort. We'd met in my senior year of high school, and the friendship looked promising. After two year's courtship, we were married on July 7, 1941. Now six years later, I found him no less thoughtful or genuine. He was not demonstrative; it was his quiet manner that I found so pleasing. Just yesterday on his lunch hour he brought me my Ivory soap, recalling from my last confinement how the hospital soap had irritated my skin.

For the past six nights I sat in a chair unable to sleep. Then the hemorrhage began, the nurses acted without delay, the doctors were summoned.

By morning the condition hadn't changed. The interne with the crew cut and engaging smile came in with his chart.

"Mrs. StCyr," he began, "a decision was reached last night. You must have a caesarian. Can you furnish names of blood donors?" I swallowed before speaking. "Yes," I answered, "my husband and three brothers—for a start."

I was made ready for surgery and wheeled down the long corridor by an orderly. At the end of the ride, the orderly touched me lightly on the shoulder to announce that my husband was there. I blinked twice to be sure. Arthur was white enough to be on a table beside me. Arthur kissed me, then moved aside.

We were in the operating room, tiled in a soft shade of green. How often I had seen that color in rooms where quiet and calm were the requisite. The massive overhead light dominated the room. I could hear the incessant flow of water for the scrubbing of hands, and I felt the same cold one feels standing by a shaded flume.

3

Nurses walked about performing their tasks with reassuring precision. One of them walked over to me to tell me my doctor had just come in. The anesthetist then performed his benevolently brief work. When I awoke I was in a small private room with a nurse insisting I be covered with the heavy brown blanket she held in her arms. I was protesting belligerently until I had to admit the nurse's advantages over mine. During the next spell of consciousness, I noticed Arthur beside me, half-smiling. "Patty-Anne is beautiful, Peg. Looks just like Gail did. Wait until you see her." Before I could respond, I was sleeping again.

A nurse dropped in to exclaim, "Congratulations! I've just seen your little girl. She is a doll!" I only wished I had the strength to sit up and have the nurse bring her in. But just the weakness in my voice, hardly rising above a whisper, convinced me that any affort would be too much. I was completely spent. "If the baby is a girl," Arthur had said in March, "why don't we name her Patty-Anne?" As if he'd thought of nothing else all day!

Now our Patty-Anne was here; Gail would have a playmate! I felt no exhilaration. I was limp and exhausted, stunned into the realization that recovery would not be automatic.

One by one in frightening succession came the life-saving apparatus, changing my room into an emergency station of some sort. The intravenous stand had already been set up opposite the transfusion bottle. Now I was watching a maintenance man wheel in an oxygen tank. Private nurses were ordered around the clock. Tubes were carefully—however uncomfortable it felt—installed in both my nostrils and forced further down. Both arms were strapped to boards at my side. Needles carried blood and intravenous feedings into my veins. I was awakened periodically for penicillin shots. Hardly fifteen minutes would pass without someone coming in to see if the oxygen, blood, or vein feeding was going right.

Finally things grew quiet. I needed to think. I could not think with all these workers in the room. As I stared up at the bottles, then down at my wrists held so firm, I tried over and over again to reason all this out. *Temporary, temporary, temporary* rang monotonously in my brain. There would be no crying; crying would only shake the tubes loose, bringing some of the uniformed staff back to put them in place, to have me gagging once again. "Save the tears," I warned myself.

No one but Mother and Arthur was allowed to visit me. Mother looked so scared when she saw me. I was glad I couldn't see myself! Arthur covered his feelings magnificently, but Mother. . . .

Hours had passed after their visit. I awoke from my sleep to the stillness of my room. I felt terribly alone. The night outside my window was so very black.

One nurse came in more often than the others. She was kind and cheerful and looked spring-fresh. Was there anything I wanted to make me more comfortable? No. I couldn't add a thank you. "I'll be back soon," she assured me. She was extremely faithful that night. The next evening I learned why; this same nurse was explaining just above a whisper to someone in my room, "She's a very sick girl. I left her side very little last night. I was afraid to leave her alone too long, but there were only two of us on duty last night. You see, the recuperating mothers here, as a rule, can get by with a minimum of attention; but your daughter is a sick girl."

5

What was Mother doing here at this late hour? Visiting hours were over, that much I knew. I opened my eyes and concentrated. The room was only dimly lit, yet I recognized the figure between the nurse and Mother. It was Eleanor, my sister, home from Boston where she worked. I stirred so she'd know I was awake and I wouldn't have to hear the nurse go into further detail. "Hi, Sis," Eleanor smiled wanely, then edged over, tenderly touching my fingertips.

"Hi." I tried to match her smile. Now, here's competition for the sick, I thought to myself.

"How are you?" she went on.

"Fine," I gasped. It was the shortest answer I could think of, about all I could spare with my limited strength.

"You look fine!" she exaggerated.

The nurse advised that this was as long as they could stay. She had already broken a rule, due to the fact that Eleanor was from out-of-town and such a close member of the family.

Just before the first private-duty nurse was expected, a young, auburn-haired, floor nurse solemnly reminded me that I was quite ill, and since she was going off duty for the weekend, asked if I wished her to call a priest. A Catholic's obligation to a Catholic!

Reality moved in beside me. The priest arrived shortly. The nurse reverently assisted in the preparations attached to the anointing of the sick. The only person I'd ever known to receive this so-final sacrament had been my Irish grandmother. I was only a child of twelve. That memory was vivid. I had been only a room away when Mother and my Aunt Agnes, faces tear-stained, remained kneeling during the anointing with oils and prayers for the dying. Grandmother was seventy-five years old. An hour following the last rites, her breathing stopped forever. I was twenty-six. I did not wish to die.

The nurse left while Father heard my confession but returned to witness the giving of communion and the anointing of my eyes, ears, nose, lips, hands and feet, while he quietly recited prayers for health of soul and body. With the lighted blessed candle she escorted the priest out of my room. An overwhelming comfort replaced my childlike trepidation. I was not going to die.

My recovery was most greatly affected by the care of Mrs. Augusta Pillsbury, a one-in-a-million kind of nurse. How tirelessly she worked to help me laugh, eat, and recover my enthusiasm for life itself. As soon as the intravenous feedings were discontinued, it became necessary to re-awaken the taste for food. My taste buds had become sluggish too. The food tasted metallic, and I couldn't have cared less. This not-caring prompted Mrs. Pillsbury, each day, to inject the subject of food in almost every conversation we had.

From now on, she insisted, she was going to cook my food herself in the hospital kitchen. She would stand by my bed, undisturbed by my continued lethargy, naming dish after dish to strike just one that might excite, all the while feeding me hot tea through an angled glass straw. I was not accustomed to being this spoiled, and I did try to discourage her. Another thing, that walk over to the kitchen was too long for a woman her age. Thirdly, what if I were unable to eat when it was put before me? She would ignore whatever I gave for an excuse. "I can get you anything you feel like eating. Remember, I was supervisor of nurses over there not *long* ago! And I fit in with the kitchen staff, still."

She never gave up until I named something from

sheer defeat. True to her word, she herself cooked it, and spoonfed me since I remained so helpless.

Finally, I began to sleep under my own power without medication. The oxygen tube was withdrawn from my nose although no one had removed the tank from my room. The last of the transfusion bottles (there had been three in all), lingered empty, still against the wall.

Chapter 2

I never stopped wondering what had caused this pregnancy to be so different from when I carried Gail. And oh the loneliness that was setting in now for that very child! She was beginning to invade my dreams at night with a presence that was unnerving, running in and out of the house, questioning, as was her natural way. She was so alive and irresistible I could almost touch her. When I'd waken from the dream, I had to fight back the tears. Arthur's visit would console me. I knew I was far from ready to be discharged, to go home. I couldn't leave my bed, even while the nurse changed the sheets! I wasn't even strong enough to hold my new baby. I guessed that was why they didn't bring her in to me. Such longing would upset me.

Every evening Arthur would look in at our Patty-Anne for us both, then describe her all over again for me, and do the same for her sister when he dropped in to my parents' home to say goodnight to her. Patty-Anne had been out of the incubator since her fourth day.

Nine days had passed since the caesarian. My doctor told Arthur it was time for him to let the third-shift and morning-shift nurses go. He felt Mrs. Pillsbury was making such strides in my behalf that Arthur would be wise to have her stay a few more days just to be on the safe side.

At 3 P.M. Esther O'Leary, the first shift nurse, shook hands with me while I thanked her sincerely for serving so well and particularly for kindling my Irish with that hardback novel of hers, *Mrs. Mike*. She laughed and winked. Every chapter had been agony. But she had never let me put it down, promising it would keep me awake and make me tired enough to sleep *at night*. Now, that's the poorest recommendation for any book I ever heard of!

It became a battle of the wills (O'Leary's and mine), before I finished that book. I threatened to lose it on her. She said she thought I had a *sense of humor*. "*Where*," I challenged, "did she find anything in that tragic story to stir a sense of humor, Irish or otherwise?"

But now, feeling better and bidding her goodbye, I recognized her philosophy: if I had someone else's grief to weep over, it would save me from weeping for my own.

On second thought, Esther O'Leary deserved an affectionate kiss, and congratulations.

Three days later, Mrs. Pillsbury announced that I was ready to go the rest of the way without her, too. I wasn't as sure about that as she was, but my doctor confirmed it.

Alone in my room shortly afterward, I let my thoughts wander to all that was good about our life. Then, turning my head in the direction of the window, I saw a daddy and two small children strolling across the hospital lawn, coming to a halt near the window of the room next to mine. He was apparently allowing his offspring a glimpse of their mother still in confinement there, and vice versa. I studied them jealously. Impetuously, the little girl flung her coat open to show off a new dress. They were so happy and lighthearted, the girl, her brother and father.

Suddenly my belated tears gushed forth. Heavy sobbing followed beyond all control. I wanted to hold my children near me. Oh, please God, *when* would I be able to leave this place and take up normal living again?

My door was ajar and I heard footsteps down the hall. Two of my friends were coming to see me now that I was no longer in critical condition. A dainty pair of soft, white-calf booties was in the first package I unwrapped. They were unbelievably tiny, but then so was our baby, Arthur had said. A pink crocheted dress with ribbon running through the bodice was peeking out of the frail tissue in the next gift box.

Arthur's mother and sister were soon greeting me from the door, and gay chatter began. The long cry was forgotten.

With visiting hours over, a nurse came in to tell me that they were bringing my baby up, did I think I would like to hold her? What did *she* think? She smiled knowingly and let the young nurse, carrying Patty-Anne, in beside me. The nurse steadied my thinned arms and bony hands. I knew I must look gaunt although I hadn't used a mirror yet. Everything had been done for me, combing, brushing, bathing. Now, with this baby to raise, I had better do something to change my condition.

I examined Patty-Anne closely. How very nice she looked . . . her face was so round, her hair was so black!

"Hasn't she nice ears?" I said, addressing the nurse.

"Indeed, she has. Now you get strong and out of here fast to take care of her."

And away she glided with my baby. With new zest I emptied my supper tray in record time.

Now two different nurses were pushing in a wheelchair. "You're going for a trial run. Doctor just called." It would be my first time out of bed and my confidence wavered. The two of them gripped me under the arms and slid me onto the chair cushioned with pillows. My body was sensitive from lying prone so long and from all the needles. I felt like a punctured daisy petal after an invasion of garden pests.

How stimulating was this ride, past all the rooms which lodged the smiling mothers pleasingly proud, boasting aptitudes of their respective offspring. For awhile I was allowed to sit in the solarium with other new mothers who were anxiously anticipating their departure. Since it was my first recess, I grew tired all too quickly and was wheeled back to my room. Arthur visited that evening and I described my pleasant afternoon journey. His tenseness seemed to be leaving him now. We shared our new enthusiasms.

Within twenty-four hours, the souvenir from my ride showed itself. A blood clot in my left leg. I had been in bed too long.

A brand new interne was back and forth all night at one-hour intervals, telling me nothing, checking the leg. Later I learned that he had been studying the course and speed of that clot. I had been puzzled why he had begun quizzing me in the first place; "Do you feel an aching anywhere—a tightening—anything? Are you sure?" It was so soon after my wheelchair ride. I was happily reflecting on that still. He was back again, after only an hour. Same questions. It bored me and I wondered if all internes started this way. "No. I feel nothing, nothing. Oh, a kind of tightening.

Yes. Where? My legs. Which leg? Both legs. I don't know! I didn't really know." I was trying not to lose patience with him. Why dwell on a mere ache after all the worrisome real trouble I'd just gotten over?

Several hours later I established that it was my left leg. Only one leg, I told him. What did it feel like? "Like after riding a bicycle for too long. You know. An aching calf-muscle!" I dismissed it.

By morning, I was again in surgery. The feeling after surgery was not so easy to shrug off as the one leading up to it. It made me wonder if I were worth salvaging. I hoped that my family would think so. As for me, I had my doubts.

That night, my brother John came to see me. His eyes were red. He looked solemn. That assured me.

John was seldom solemn. As children, we two were inseparable, never in disagreement. He had laughing blue eyes and a ready wit. He wasn't using it now. I guess you can label that love.

"I didn't know you cared!" I said, to relieve his embarrassment. "Just a little," he replied. Then he told me a secret. His wife Sylvia was pregnant. First child. "We're not telling anyone yet," he warned. It thrilled me. Our garden of cousins would grow. I thought, "If I can hurry and get well, I shall write a verse about them." Whenever something touched me deeply I would sit down and compose rhythmic lines, then tuck them in a drawer somewhere in the house. Arthur would receive one on almost every birthday or one of our anniversaries. Light, light-verse. But the only words right now that concerned me, poetic or otherwise, were those that would impart just *when* I would be discharged from this hospital.

They blessedly came—after 23 days! An eternity had passed.

"Now you must get plenty of sunshine and all the

eggnogs you can drink," said my doctor. "You have the summer to build yourself up. What you do in these next months will have a great deal to do with your physical strength in the future, Mrs. StCyr."

I couldn't think of a remark, so I made none.

He went on, "I am sorry that we can't let you take the baby with you just yet. She dropped some of her birthweight and we must put it back on her before you can safely take her home." That made good sense to me. As I stared down at my bony arms and hands, I was alarmingly aware of my present fragility. The leg, too, was very swollen now, pulling painfully, and I had two incisions to heal. Well, at least my baby and I had come through it. The rest would seem far more easy.

"At last," my doctor was saying, "we have the answers to explain your abnormal bleeding and all things leading up to it." I straightened up in my bed. "Your family will be limited now to these two children." No matter how softly a doctor announces this sentence, it echoes cruel. "The pathologist has just given us his findings. The tissues from the diseased uterus we removed proved beyond all doubt that you had something that up to now we know too little about. It is something called endometriosis."

I stopped him. "Endo-*what*?"

"Endo-me-tri-osis," he sounded it out patiently. I tried to repeat it after him, but I was impatient to hear it fully explained. "It is an ailment of the endometrium, the lining of the uterus. The extensive hemorrhaging you suffered was caused by the rupturing of this membrane. In your advanced case this organ was so beyond repair that it had to be removed. Because you are so young, we acted conservatively to spare you surgical menopause. The pathologist's findings suggest that endometriosis may also affect your remaining

14

organs, in which case you will recognize the symptoms in time. Either surgery or x-ray treatments will be employed to remedy your trouble. Either hemorrhaging or that by-now familiar pain will be your warning."

In my throat I felt a choking again.

"I have already explained all this to your husband."

"Thank you, Doctor," I said. I did not wish to hear any more. I wished to be spared from the serious and unalterable.

My doctor patted my hand. It made me feel little, but big indeed were my dreams of going home.

"You are fortunate to have had children at all, Mrs. StCyr," said the doctor before he left. I kept remembering that while the nurses helped me to get into the royal-blue maternity dress I had worn into the hospital; little thought had been given to what I would wear home.

I was taken to the exit by wheelchair, with Arthur and Dad at each side of me carrying my overnight case, gifts and cards. The day supervisor of nurses rose from her desk as I was being wheeled out. She smiled, saying, "We never thought you'd be taken out of here alive, Mrs. StCyr." For a while, no one had, I judged. All the convalescent cards and prayer enrollments I had received; so little of my mail contained baby congratulatory messages!

Gail was waiting at the walk as Arthur pulled the car up close to the concrete steps. She seemed perplexed at how much help I needed to reach her grandmother's door. Gail looked as though she were trying hard to remember me. My chin was quivering at mere sight of her, as she was lifted to a sitting position atop the kitchen table, making it easier for me to hug her and feel her warm body against mine. God is so good, I whispered to myself.

While Arthur fixed a chair for me with pillows and

a second one to hold the leg that ached now from standing too long, my father prepared my first eggnog, slipping in a drop of good brandy. Louis Nordle would have a bottle of liquor last anywhere from a year to two, keeping it for strictly medicinal purposes.

My Scandinavian Dad! For as long as I could remember, he was the family eggnog artist in this big house where his children had been born and nursed through the mumps, measles and other childhood ailments.

"You look better already," Arthur said, after I settled in the familiar family chair.

Gail added, "I will help you, Mommy. I will help you. Won't I, Grammy?"

"She sure will," answered Mother with her eyes beaming. Gail had been her very first grandchild and therefore very special. From the time she was a mere six weeks old, she was borrowed all too often. My father would wear Arthur and me down, saying over and over throughout the summer, "That's a hot apartment for a baby. Too hot, too hot!" We would somehow come to believe him. Then, after the second day, our baby's absence would have us dejected and we would go running to reclaim her.

Now, Gail's own longing for her new sister needed to be answered. Baby Patty-Anne was having her strength built up. It would not take long, we explained. Gail accepted our answers.

She was endearingly sweet in the many days at my parents' home. Hobbling about on the swollen, sensitive leg, I could find her most frequently tagging along behind me when I attempted to make our beds or to do some other light chore. It required so much of my very limited strength. Recovery remained slow. But my little three-year old would insist on helping me pull up a spread, or carry clothes from one room to another each morning while her grandmother prepared breakfast.

By the time two weeks had passed, I could see Mother looking quite drawn. With Arthur joining us for supper and my bachelor sister and brother home on weekends, it made for a crowded household. Even with Eleanor's help, the extra cooking alone was a strain. Mother had worked hard all her life raising her five children and she needed rest right now. Despite Mother's objections, I insisted on returning to our nearby two-story frame cottage, to try to resume my role as housewife and mother. The thought sent waves of happiness through me!

The actuality was sheer bliss. When I walked into my kitchen, with Gail's feet beating me there, its emptiness struck me. I turned on the radio and inspected every room as though I had never seen it before. How perfectly Edgar A. Guest phrased it when he wrote: "Ye sometimes have t' roam afore ye really 'preciate the things ye lef' behind, an' hunger for 'em somehow with 'em allus on yer mind. It takes a heap o' *livin'* in a house to make it HOME!" Here was ours, where Arthur had painted the walls, and I had added burgundy and beige drapes and wallpaper to make the dining and living room companionable.

Arthur's breakfast dishes were waiting in the sink. Poor Arthur. These weeks had been so hectic for him, racing home from work, going to supper at Mother's, back home to dress up to visit me at the hospital, remembering whatever little notions I needed him to bring me, then back to kiss his little girl goodnight. He, too, was tired.

Gail went upstairs to her bedroom to bring down a few of the toys she had missed. In the dust on top of the deep linen chest, I frivolously wrote the date, June 18, 1947, confirming its mistress's return. I raised the nearby window to let in the pleasant June air, turned on the small radio to invite other voices, and dusted all the sills and table tops. I could have no way of knowing how soon our Patty-Anne would be coming home, but from this moment on I was going to gradually increase my work routine to make myself ready for her. I would be careful. And of course God would be here to help me. My leg still made me tired, but I was home, home, home.

I'd been at it a few days, swinging the broom and beginning the preparations for meals with Arthur taking over when he reached home. In our new gratitude, these small chores seemed like such very big privileges. Then came the hospital call, saying that our baby was ready to be brought home. Mixed feelings arose within me. Extreme happiness, followed by pangs of fear. Happy again, then frightened. It was morning, and we were requested to be at the hospital by noon.

Gail's ecstasy at the good news helped to buoy me. Together, she and I stacked the lower bathinette shelf with diapers, powder, oil, shirts and nighties. Thoughts, all positive, began to race through my mind. Baby Patty-Anne would now be exclusively in our care. Here in this very house.

Rose, my brother Louie's wife, carried the baby clothes and the new white-fringed shawl as we walked slowly into the hospital and on down to the nursery.

With the nurse assisting as we dressed the baby, we noticed especially then how little our Patty-Anne was. The face which had been solid and firm was touched with wrinkles. It was evident how much attention she would require. Fortunate that we would have the summer months in which to put the pink back into her pallid cheeks.

Before she was fully dressed, Patty-Anne lifted her lids to reveal two very dark brown eyes. She scrutinized her abductors with a long and steady gaze.

Responsibility for this tiny baby was ample reason for overlooking one's own weakness. I began to thrive on the heavy schedule. Mother dropped in to help, often to be disappointed in the little left for her to do. Close-by, she would find baby resting serenely in the ribbon-bedecked crib sent down by her paternal grandmother.

Our hospital and medical bills finally reached us. When Arthur and I worriedly sat down to total them, we turned pale at the stark figure of $1,028! To pay the private nurse fees, we had already withdrawn our entire savings from the bank. Our income for the year was to come to only $2,797.69 *before* taxes. We pondered how long it would take to pay all this.

Wearing her sister's christening dress, Patty-Anne was baptized in the little ivy-covered chapel where Arthur and I had been married. Our two closest friends, Roger and Stella Letendre, came up from Lincoln, Massachusetts to act as Godparents. Watching Roger's quiet solicitude giving birth to nervous gestures, apparent as we walked into the sacristy just behind him, we wanted to whisper that it was not the Hope Diamond he was guarding. But as we lovingly glanced into the shawl-covered bundle resting in Stella's arms, we admitted that she was almost as tiny and every bit as precious.

That whole summer was spent counting our blessings and diapers swaying merrily on the line. We watched Patty-Anne's legs and doll-size arms grow tan from her naps in the sun, and we were grateful.

Chapter 3

"The first year in a premie's life is not like that of other babies," said our friends and family over and over again.

On Patty-Anne's first birthday she weighed only sixteen pounds. While she held her head erect at two months and goo'd and gaa'd at four and one-half months, laughed real heartily at six months, I had pitifully little to record in the pages of her baby book. Gail's progress had been so rapid, that I hadn't the time to record everything in her book.

Patty-Anne's first tooth came through at nine and one-half months and the rest followed close behind. As she approached her second birthday, we were growing less and less confident that her development, though late, was promising.

The very first sound after the goo and gaa was a long awaited thrill. The music of it reached our ears as Gail skipped in to greet Patty over her crib one morning. Patty reciprocated with an excited "Gay" for Gail. Jubilantly we brought her downstairs and sat her in her highchair while we each celebrated with a hearty breakfast. Patty-Anne had baby cereal and milk. She held her spoon nicely and needed very little assistance. Her arm motion seemed good.

We were disappointed by her complete indifference to any toy handed her. Her Christmas gifts were ignored. Arthur and I noticed that never once did she move from a prone position on our living room floor where we placed her on our cotton quilt. She was nineteen months old!

It was on a Sunday afternoon when one of our visitors curiously attempted to maneuver Patty-Anne forward that Arthur and I became silently and simultaneously convinced that we could no longer avoid exploring the truth. Any encouragement given our baby to move from any suggested point went unrewarded. She could not advance. She could not crawl. She was unable to command her legs and other parts to take her anywhere.

That very evening after Gail and Patty-Anne were tucked in asleep, Arthur and I painfully voiced our rising premonitions. Talking made them even bleaker. We recalled her consistently fragile condition, so susceptible to colds during the bad weather that hardly four or five days elapsed without medicines. And why did we, so often, need to take turns sitting up with her at night to help her breathe easier?

Up to now, we had been trying to think only of the brighter side of things, the crisis of her birth and my own good recovery. And although we were able to pay only a little at a time on those bills that had resulted, they were reducing some.

But recently there had been added the worry of our first child. Gail's tonsils had started giving her trouble. After several weeks of Gail's waking in the night with sorely aching arms and legs, and watching her slip into a general run-down condition, Arthur and I began to fear rheumatic causes. After careful examination, the doctor calmed our fears, proposing that since summer was not too far off and could bring relief, we should wait until its end to decide the wisest course.

With one child feverish and another plagued by constantly aching legs and arms, Arthur and I kept our vigil. Giving medicines to each at appointed hours and rubbing Gail's wretched limbs, we had less time to give to the woeful concern of Patty-Anne's slow development.

During that particular year, Arthur and I grew more than in all the previous seven years. We sat at our respective posts nursing these girls, by now wise enough not to speak our troubled minds. It was here we learned the value of glance over the spoken word; unlimited feeling conveyed by an understanding glance flashed in the recipient's direction. Congratulatory, sympathetic, and even comical appreciation. Little could we know how much of that would enrich our lives!

Patty-Anne's only entertainment was watching the gay performance of adults dancing before her. She would give the "raspberries" with her puckered lips, quite expertly, and throw her arms and legs about excitedly. Following this phase, she became interested in toy animals. The only other thing capturing her interest was Gail's best doll. What magnificent response she gave to the unexpected sight of that! She would squeal and stiffen until Gail brought it to her.

Like all parents who lean on hope, we were tremendously happy in early January to notice Patty-

Anne in her corduroy creepers move forward a pace or two on the rug. She was creeping slowly and laboriously.

Early the following month on two successive evenings, Patty-Anne vomited slightly before I changed her for bed. Since no other symptoms were present, we blamed it on her teething. One tooth was not quite through, stubbornly holding back.

On the third morning at breakfast she refused food. I bathed and dressed her, then noticed signs of fever. The thermometer showed a reading of 103°. I laid her down only long enough to clear the kitchen table, then returned to her with a bit of orange juice which she also rejected. I then gave her medication to bring down the fever and continued holding her in my arms while she dozed restlessly.

Then suddenly I noticed her stiffen. Her eyes rolled back. She lost consciousness. Her breathing was strange. Her face twitched grotesquely and her arms and legs jerked mechanically.

Gail was playing outside. I was alone, terrified. I was certain that my baby was dying. *But, God, you can't take her from us. You just can't. She is the last we shall have. And we've had her less than two years! Please. We can't lose her.* Why must this *be? All three of us need her.*

I paced frantically from one room to another, clutching my sick baby, praying more desperately than ever before. I couldn't think what I must do.

Mother. I must phone Mother. I couldn't remember the doctor's number. I could not let my baby down to free my hands to look for it. But I could ring Mother's number from memory.

Soon she was in my kitchen. Gail trailed behind her having caught a glimpse of her from the backyard where she was at play. Unusually calm for Mother,

24

she quietly assured me that my baby was not dying, that she could almost promise me this was a convulsion from which Patty-Anne would pull through in a few minutes. She then walked reassuredly to the phone and called our doctor.

Just before the pediatrician arrived, a little cry broke the terrifying silence. Patty-Anne was conscious though spent and colorless.

Dr. D examined her and announced that she had a slight case of pneumonia and that the convulsion was induced by the high fever. He prescribed penicillin. The second blank he filled was for a sedative which we were to keep on hand for any future seizure that might occur. This would shorten its duration. Patty-Anne slept for some time after that as the doctor had predicted she would.

The whole miserable episode seemed a climax to the past long months of anguish. Things couldn't get any worse, we told ourselves that night.

Finally, the rough winter was over. An appointment was arranged at the Orthopedic Clinic in the hospital where Patty was born. It was for a Tuesday morning, three days after Patty's second birthday.

It was a beautiful spring morning. I went by bus while Mother kept Gail for me at her house. Arthur wouldn't be able to leave work to drive me.

As the bus rolled along, I couldn't help but notice all the healthy little toddlers without their jackets romping up and down their front lawns. Like Gail, they were occupying the long days while impatiently awaiting school-age, filled with envy of the older neighboring children. A child's world. A child's wishing.

By this time I had become afraid to wish. So had Arthur. Just this morning, along with his kiss before leaving for work, he wished me good luck, but added solemnly that he would be praying.

We reached the clinic and announced our identity. I waited with Patty-Anne in my arms. I lifted off her silk bonnet and matching nile green sweater. Other mothers waited with children of various ages, their ailments none too apparent. When our name was called I picked up the sweater and bonnet from the empty seat where I had placed them and with my baby in my arms I followed the nurse until she stopped at the desk of a kindly unassuming middle-aged woman.

"Won't you sit down, Mrs. StCyr?" she said smiling. And to Patty-Anne, "Hello, Patricia. Well, aren't you a sweet little girl!" "I'm Miss B, Mrs. StCyr, and I'll need some information before we can proceed with the examinations. How old is Patricia?"

"Two years old last week." I began nervously.
"Any other children?"

"Yes, another daughter, five years old."

"Is she well? Any abnormalities, as compared to her sister's slow development?" she asked systematically with her eyes on her pencil.

"She is normal; no trouble whatsoever." I answered, thankfully. (I felt foolish bringing up the subject of such a common thing as tonsillitis. Today, here, it seemed so irrelevant.)

"Any peculiarity about Patricia's birth?" she queried with eyes squarely meeting mine.

"Yes, too many" I sighed. "Premature birth by caesarian section."

Her eyebrows lifted. She waited for me to continue.

"Abnormal surrounding conditions later described by my doctor to be endometriosis. He said it had been a long time developing. The uncontrollable hemorrhaging was what necessitated the baby's premature delivery."

"And with your first baby it was a normal birth?" she questioned.

"Yes," I replied.

With all this jotted down, she asked me to describe the last two years more explicitly. I shut out all emotion in order to give an accurate account. I no longer wished to postpone what Arthur and I must learn.

She thanked me, then referred me to a woman pediatrician clad in tailored navy-blue gabardine who spoke with faultless diction. In an everything-will-be-all right voice, she asked, "And how is Patricia this nice spring morning?"

Not able to match her cheerfulness and feeling there was little to smile about, I answered with difficulty, "Quite well this morning."

Holding the data in her hands, she asked, "Would you kindly undress Patricia so that we might get the check-up underway?"

While I sat with Patty-Anne on my lap, the dark-haired professional woman listened to my baby's heartbeat, looked at her eyes, her ears, her throat, then instructed me to leave Patty-Anne in her underwear to permit examination by the next doctor. While we waited, she completed her portion of the forms asking about Patty's general ailments, which shots she had received, what vitamins she was on and how well she ate.

"You will now see Dr. J who is the orthopedic specialist." With another smile she walked out the door with purpose in each step. Other small patients were on the morning's agenda.

Patty-Anne grew restless and started to whimper. A young man in a white coat sauntered in, whistling an airy tune. He now carried the chart on which Patty-Anne's case history was recorded. Apprehension was increasing as I waited between each examiner. I felt no hope of leaving here with good news. But because this man's whistle resembled Arthur's which I'd missed hearing lately, I momentarily relaxed. He wore white shoes with brown crepe soles, I noticed, as he lifted his weight up to rest on the black leather examination table. He did not hurry into technical data. He ignored the chart and asked things about Patty-Anne unrelated to those already asked. While he questioned, he gently moved her legs into a number of positions, several times sending a quaint whistle through his teeth for her entertainment. Then after rolling her over once again, he tried lifting her chest off the table where she lay prone. While some of the exercises, particularly the stretching of what I now know as the heelcord, brought forth a little cry, his peculiar whistling held her entranced.

The young man's nurse-secretary unobtrusively walked in to take his diagnosis down in shorthand. He was reporting his findings in long medical terms which were all foreign to me. Until these terms were translated into layman's language, I would not allow myself to get upset.

He then asked his secretary to bring in a prominent nerve specialist who also served in this clinic. The latter doctor was an older and more serious personality. Patty-Anne cried as he tapped her knees and elbows with his rubber hammer. Ignoring this, he exchanged thoughts with Dr. J in more of the strange language, then left to see the next patient.

Once this information was down Dr. J dismissed his nurse and asked me to dress my baby. Toying with the chart he held thoughtfully between his fingers, he said slowly, "Well, Mrs. StCyr, your baby has spastic paralysis in her lower extremities. It is a type of cerebral palsy caused by damage to some part of the brain about the time of her birth."

My heart began to beat rapidly. Muscles of my stomach contracted and my blood seemed to heat up. "This accounts for Patricia's hindrance to motor control and her retardation of speech."

He didn't stop. "You see, there are three main message centers in the brain. Each center receives and sends the messages necessary for each particular function of the body. Damage to any of the brain cells can be compared to broken down telephone lines for which emergency lines must be called upon to carry messages though." After a short breath, "This however is the long way around. So it is with the spastic child in order for him to command the performance of his muscles."

"It will be your work, Mrs. StCyr, under the guidance of therapists at our local rehabilitation center, to help train your child in her difficult pursuits, despite damaged cells. It will be far from easy. Results will not be quickly realized. Not in days or weeks or months. It will take years and will require a great deal of perseverance."

As he finished his sigh of relief went unstifled.

I sat staring at him, unable to voice intelligent response. No physical pain ever compared to this. With a fist resting gravely against his chin, he sat waiting to answer any questions I might have. But the shock left no room for questions. I felt only grief. No one could erase the facts. The words kept playing back in my ears, "brain damage, not weeks, not months, years."

He held his chart limply and his eyes offered help. But I had nothing to ask. I doubted that he had omitted anything. If he had, I well knew this would be enough for my husband and me for quite some time to come.

I was glad for my baby's shoes to lace. This done, I mechanically picked up my handbag. I held Patty-Anne in my weakened arms. Dr. J slowly let himself off the table to hold the door open saying softly, "I will arrange your appointment for registration at the rehab center, Mrs. StCyr, and one of its staff will mail you your letter of admission."

On the corner, I got in the bus, dropping my token into the coin box. I wanted most to be alone. Oblivious of the few passengers, but fully aware of the several empty seats, I walked pensively to the rear of the coach where I was least likely to be intruded upon.

How would I tell Arthur what I had just learned? I had but a few hours to review our plight. I had to pick up Gail at Mother's. On second thought, maybe it would be better to ask Mother to keep Gail longer so that I might be free to concentrate on when and how to tell him.

At Mother's I sat only long enough to make my request and the promise to let her know the outcome of my trip a little later. Understandingly, she said, "Of course." I don't believe my face yet betrayed how serious it was.

I prepared a lunch for Patty-Anne and myself, then put her upstairs for a short nap. I went through the motions of my neglected morning chores while she slept and found the employment of my hands soothing.

While I worked, I recalled how smoothly our early years of marriage had run. Three excitingly happy years. Proud of our new furnishings, we had pooled our efforts each Saturday straightening out the apartment, rewarding ourselves by evening with a good movie or dancing to a big-name band. Until we were blessed with the promise of our first child, my secretarial job helped us build a small bank account. Arthur's job was in the Transportation Department as a civilian employee at the Grenier Air Force Base just outside of town. We lived at the apartment until Gail reached seven months and it was no longer feasible to squeeze playpen, crib, and bathinette into honeymoon quarters. Since summers in the city make one dream about the cool outskirts, we impatiently awaited the suburban rental soon to be vacated. A bit nostalgically, we left the place where we began as man and wife.

It was more serious adjusting to a large house, and it was funny remembering how crushed we had felt upon discovering the miracle necessary to make a six-room house cozy with only three rooms of furniture! Once we recovered from the initial letdown, we went about renovating old pieces and learning the magic of a paintbrush. We applied luminous stars to the sloped ceiling of Gail's bedroom to hasten her journeys to Nod, and Arthur built a fence to limit her daytime travels to our own front yard. Our cottage was situated directly on a highway bearing heavy traffic of vacationers to our scenic New Hampshire lakes and mountains.

Throughout the day I had listened to my daughter's happy play with her imaginary playmate, a common practice with children who have no others in the neighborhood. A child makes a day so handsomely full. I would sew pretty things for her, while she played contentedly. In the late summer, we'd vacation at a Maine beach. Our plans were seldom interrupted. I was mistress of my day's routine and Arthur was contented with his. After today, all of that would change.

By the time Patty-Anne awakened I was in more comforted spirit, thinking that this perhaps was why God had allowed us so many carefree moments. I had a slightly better perspective with which to greet my husband.

Patty-Anne smiled for him and soon I asked if he'd mind going after Gail while I finished preparations for our evening meal. He freshened up after he returned with Gail, helping her to do the same. We then sat down to the table. To postpone the ordeal at least until our meal was over, I attempted conversation pertaining to his day. But he seemed to lack enthusiasm for that subject. Before dessert was served, his meal only half eaten, his anxious drawn face indicating the strain he'd been under that whole day, he said:

"Let's have it, Peg."

If I thought my composure of the last hour would support me through this, it was strictly because I had not realized that I would be unable to deliver the hurt to him without flinching myself. I wanted to hurry through it while I could hold together. Nevertheless, it must be the complete story just as I had received it.

Amazed at all I remembered despite the pain of it, I recited the words without break, now understanding the doctor's purpose in so doing. I studied my husband as he ate what was left on his plate. He was not enjoying his food, only camouflaging his anxiety. I described the orthopedic examination and felt every bit of his heartache.

Exactly as I had myself, Arthur made no verbal response. He was swallowing it hard, defeated by its severity. We had both hoped that whatever ailed our daughter we would learn of a positive cure. But just as I had been told, I explained to Arthur that we could minimize its handicaps with conscientious effort and thereby help Patty-Anne make the most of whatever skills might be discovered in her. For now, the prime concern should be her physical development.

"May I have another coffee, please," he asked. The harassing assignment was over. I refilled his cup, knowing that my husband would live up to this new obligation just as he had every other one.

Gail shifted in her chair, bored by subject matter far beyond her five years. We suggested that she play outside while dishes were removed from the table for washing and drying. Dusk for her hadn't yet come.

For the balance of the evening Arthur was silent. I could understand, reliving my own afternoon. Were his reflections following the same vein as had my own those very first hours after hearing the diagnosis? What *was* going on underneath the flesh of a man who had twice tied extensions to the light pulls and applied adhesive to the scatter rugs, to protect his pregnant wife?

Conversation would not have lightened our sorrow. What could we have said? The unchanging would be our love for each other. This, combined with faith, would have to sustain our small foursome. We would need to live each day one day at a time.

We went to bed. "God help us to learn and labor through it for the sake of our child."

Chapter 4

*W*aking up each morning after that initial clinic visit was painful. There was the reminder all over again that our two-year old was cruelly afflicted.

Somewhere I picked up a pamphlet on cerebral palsy. On its cover was an artist's sketch of one of its victims. The face was contorted and the hands turned up with crooked fingers bent like claws. That sent shivers through me because our Patty-Anne didn't look anything like this. She looked so normal. But did this mean she would *eventually* look that way?

We had, neither one of us, ever known anyone who was cerebral-palsied. Many torturous fears plagued us. Sleep was the only time we breathed easily.

Two weeks later we received the promised letter advising us that we had been given Tuesday and Thursday afternoons for therapy treatments. The rehabilitation center was located at the very south end of our neighboring city. It would necessitate my taking the B&M (Boston & Maine) bus into the city terminal and transferring to a city transit from there to the therapy center which was three hundred feet in from the street.

The building was a light green stucco affair with brown trim. The newly landscaped grounds offered a view of the city's west side. In the far distance you could see the tall steeples of several churches and St Anselm's College high on the hill.

Inside we were approached by a beautifully coif-fured matron smartly dressed and wearing a faintly familiar cologne. I told her who we were and that our appointment was for two o'clock. She courteously bade us to be seated until Miss Stanton, the physio-therapist, was ready for us. It was a small office with an appointment schedule pinned up on the pastel wall. At the opposite side of the office stood a showcase of arts and crafts made by the handicapped; little gifts of wood, some handknit articles and hand-stitched things. While I was marvelling at the skills and won-dering about the extent of such handicaps, I was in-terrupted by the receptionist's announcement that Miss Stanton's patient was now leaving and I could take Patty-Anne in.

I walked with my baby into a huge room, parts of which were partitioned off and draped for lamp or pool treatments. A mattress lay on the floor be-yond the therapist's desk. A wide ladder leaned against the wall at the head of the mattress—for purpose of practice I supposed as steps were built at each end of a four-foot raise with sturdy rails for hand support.

Almost as if she'd met Patty-Anne before, Miss Mary Stanton smiled warmly and handed her a stuffed doll clothed in blue and orange gingham. She couldn't have chosen a more suitable enticement. Patty-Anne delightedly reached out her arms to embrace the chubby little doll before her.

Miss Stanton led us into a room beyond the one I studied so carefully. This one was much smaller and more private. Nursery plaques graced the walls and toys were scattered here and there. Patty-Anne wasn't the least shy. Loving every one who loved her, she went willingly to Miss Stanton's arms and became very interested in the therapist, as the latter went through therapeutical maneuvers with a rag doll lying on the table. She held Patty-Anne in her left arm and was in no hurry to begin on her new patient. She held no conversation with me. It took me some time to learn how many patients fill a day at such a center and how much must be accomplished in the short forty-five minutes allotted.

Miss Stanton described to Patty-Anne very intelligently how she was trying to make the lazy doll walk. Patty-Anne was all for it. I learned that "Anne" would be dropped to hasten all that was really necessary and important. Everyone on the staff after that sounded our baby's name like a musical note.

By the time the therapist transferred all her attentions to Patty's own legs after unlacing the shoes, Patty began to cry endlessly. I could do nothing. The newness of everything plus the effort exerted to get her here made me now suddenly very tired.

The day was hot and I sympathized with the therapist who remained calm through Patty's wailing. Knowing that the stretching of the heel cord caused some pain, I couldn't help feeling strained. Half the period was devoted to acclimating the child to these new surroundings so we were not forced to withstand the crying for too long. Patty was returned to me.

I didn't know the schedule for the city buses and was grateful that there was no need to rush in getting home. Gail was accustomed to staying with her Grammy whenever errands kept me in town.

We waited patiently across the street until the red and white bus came. I sat Patty close to me on the seat, my arms tired from standing with her so long. Summer heat was not for me. It was about three-quarters of a mile to the stop where I connected with the B&M bus directed north. It was a long wait between. Here again it was out of the question for Arthur to take off from work twice a week to drive me to and from such appointments. Furthermore, we couldn't have stood the hourly financial loss. Our indebtedness for Patty's birth, not to mention doctor visits and filled prescriptions, kept us continually cautious. A budget was impossible. We were still paying for the fuel of last winter, let alone saving for the next. And Arthur was considering changing to different and higher-paying work.

Patty's beaming face made up for all that her existence involved. Both Arthur's family and mine felt so affectionately toward her. Her smile radiated joy to all who saw her, the smile which inspired her grandfather to nickname her "Sunshine" which he persisted in calling her until his last days. Gail found delight in amusing her.

That summer was so hot that breezes were something only wished for. To arrange for an earlier-than-usual lunch hour, to have both of us dressed and ready for the 12:40 P.M. bus, it became a mad race accomplishing my morning's work. By fall I was forced to admit that I just could not make it any longer at the same hour. My request for a change in appointment time was immediately understood by the staff and we were given a later time. Their cheerful handling of things always served as a comfort to me. Mrs. Frances Fitzgerald, executive-secretary there, was never too busy to greet parents or to offer constructive advice on any of the problems arising.

Patty didn't get over her crying whenever she anticipated her treatments at the center for a long time. Our arrival was always heralded before we entered the door. She loved the bus rides, but the moment the driver left us off at the center and she sighted the green stucco, she would, as if to a maestro's raised baton, begin her unhappy rendition.

Once in the place, we usually had ten minutes or so to wait. I would notice Patty looking about for one she particularly loved down there: John, the Dutch caretaker. His presence always lightened the strain of our visits. His sense of humor made it impossible to detect whether his tales were fact or fiction. Most of them pertained to experiences back in Holland. More often than not I discovered that his stories were mere jest. Patty's respect for this man, I always believed, was born of his resemblance to her own grandfather.

The only serious word John ever uttered in the several years we went there was at the start. Watching Patty struggle yards away with the therapist's help, John looked over at me and said, "Do you think there's a God up there to let little ones be burdened like that?"

I wanted not to answer him, for it was our family faith, most surely, which was holding us up. But then it was John's genuine compassion that prompted his remark. Could a man of wit possibly doubt the will of God? More particularly, the existence of God?

"Yes, John, I *know* there's a God up there." And I knew my answer to be grossly inadequate; we had such a long way to go ourselves, as parents, before we could attempt to reassure doubting strangers.

*H*ow much more tolerable were my trips once the season cooled. By now, my youngest brother worked a three-to-eleven evening schedule and voluntarily taxied us to our appointments. One way made easy. Shortly after, Arthur himself went on such a shift and while it was ideal in relaxing Patty to have her Daddy drive her there, we enjoyed it very shortly. He was changed to mornings again.

Things are seldom made easy when you most need them, and the road can seem so very long! My frustration increased with the heavier schedule and domestic responsibilities still facing me when I returned home.

During therapies, Patty seldom cried. This was some relief. After awhile I learned that it was uniforms which made our baby anxious. She was always so amiable with people who didn't wear them. Much later I noticed her lack of trust in hairdressers because of their white uniforms.

Learning the exercises and going through them with the therapist for correction or approval was the chief occupation of those first months. Occupational therapy had now been added to Patty's program and while she attempted new exercises on the legs and body, Miss Stanton would invite me to watch.

Autumn was almost over when our family physician decided on a tonsillectomy for Gail. When Thanksgiving dinner was over we drove her into Manchester to the hospital. Cheering her up for the ordeal was no easier than preparing Patty for her therapy appointments.

When it was over, all our tenderness went out to Gail, fussing over her until the soreness was gone. Throughout the winter we noticed much improvement and less susceptibility to colds.

Speech therapy was added to Patty's program. Occupational therapy would teach motor control, train muscles used in hand activities, encourage the eyes and hands to work together.

Watching these cheerful therapists, I appreciated their patience with abounding admiration. They were faithfully expectant while working with their patients, never hurrying. So many vocations would certainly have been easier. Today, it was taking so long for one little boy I watched to place one tiny part of the wood pony where it belonged to form its complete outline. He was trying so laboriously to guide his fingers to maneuver the piece into its proper place. His troubles were multiple. But here in this room were tools to help him. Several hand-made pieces custom-built to answer his needs; fabric with large buttons and button holes, belts and buckles and zippers to train self-dressing, large wooden toy shoes to teach lacing and always a few rag dolls or toys carelessly thrown somewhere to invite the timid child. The colors used in the chairs, tables, cabinet doors and shelves were typically a child's. They created a happy background for arduous work.

Without having seen such a workroom, Patty's Uncle Tim showed unusual insight in the gifts he brought the following Christmas. Tim found toys that seemed designed for children like her. We had combed every toy department in town for something special, simple enough to hold her interest and at the same time promote muscle control. Tim brought a toy xylophone, a hammer and peg set to employ her more vigorously, and lastly, a fine little five-piece animal puzzle made of durable hardwood in vibrant colors. We hadn't realized there were such puzzles on the market, since those we had noticed at the Center were hand-made.

Our toys included a little station wagon with six little wooden passengers, each a different color, to be taken out and replaced again, (for hand grasp and release). The second was a sailboat on wheels with four wooden soldiers having removable heads, hats and bodies. The last was a tub in which stood three little fat men.

I discovered what extra patience and composure I must acquire in helping Patty fit these pieces in their proper place. I felt keenly her indifference to occupation such as this. Out of my own curiosity, I allowed some of the visiting children to put these toys together, discovering that one cannot judge the time required for the spastic's endeavors by that of the normal child. Thus I was goaded on to give my very best to reduce the difference for our Patty.

I allowed no interruptions after we began. To remain tranquil while overlooking so much of what I was previously able to do with my time, was *my* rehabilitation.

Fatigue threatened periodically. I was carrying Patty too long in my arms. I felt it most when I carried her down the fourteen steps to the kitchen. I often feared that both of us would fall before reaching the foot of the stairs. Sometimes I sat down on one of the steps long enough to relax before going the balance of the way. Most summer evenings, Arthur worked overtime so that I had to take Patty up again myself. When I felt I'd reached my limit physically, I slowed down on some of the lesser important therapies. This neglect always hurt more than any of the overlooked domestic chores.

42

One Sunday evening while snow gently fell outside our window, Arthur happily beckoned me to the living room where he was reading his papers beside Patty's playpen. Watching two happy faces, I listened to Arthur telling me how Patty had pulled herself up on the pen, gripping the bars, and on her toes had stepped along slowly, but *stepped*. Observing our excitement over this, she folded her hands and with bent elbows, squeezed her arms to her body and smiled a continuous smile, apparently proud of herself. This particular manner of expressing her happiness was now familiar to us.

Since the previous May, she was saying sounds which we interpreted as ma-ma, da-da, but they were spoken so weakly that we couldn't be sure. "Itha, Itha" followed next, which we felt was Patty's new name for *sister*. Then we were thrilled hearing her argue with the kitten when he grabbed her wooden spools and poked them swiftly along the floor with his front paw. "Mine, mine" she could be heard asserting herself to the playful kitten. Now she was two and one-half years old. She was crawling quite steadily and was able to get herself into a kneeling position.

One day on my return from a dental appointment, I went to Grammy's to pick up Patty and in breathless excitement Grammy was describing how our baby had attempted her first staircase to reach the upstairs bedrooms! Another happy day.

And at home, Patty could now sit erect without a back support. We were pleased also to notice a rising interest in simple toys. She followed Gail's suggestions alertly.

About this time, we invested in a home gym set. It was of sturdy construction and we traveled twenty-two miles to the small office through which they handled mail orders exclusively. This company engaged strictly in door-to-door selling in Massachusetts. We convinced them of our special need and they made exception to sell us one. It had special coated hangers for the swing and gym bar to be gripped to the indoor casings. It was very entertaining for Patty and a wonderful pastime for colder winter months, her play being so limited. The rings included in the set also did much for her. She gained confidence on the seat of the swing and from that developed the courage to attempt the rings with our help. She was still not walking, but we were grateful for what this set accomplished in exercising her muscles.

Chapter 5

*I*n the spring Arthur made us a set of parallel bars similar to ones used at the Center. They were excellent for gait training on the long cement walk outside or on rainy days inside. His next project was a standing table. Copied from the model at the Center, this was used as a support in keeping the child in a standing position. An enclosure was built from the height of Patty's back waist down to the floor with a separator between the legs. This was for the purpose of keeping the feet apart—another correctional device. In this standing position, weak leg muscles would be strengthened. While she was in the table, I brought the educational toys to her, working alongside her if she herself did not show interest.

I now realistically distinguished between the necessary and the less important jobs about the house. With housekeeping first, and home therapy second, Patty became listless, neither cooperative nor happy. The most necessary requirement was the child's willing response. After weeks of trying different hours of the day, I decided that 9:00 A.M. was best for both of us. We were then both rested and least distracted.

I would not say that dishes and dust weren't terribly disturbing, but I felt that these early years would be the ones when any kind of training could best be established. Postponing it in favor of my housework robbed me of all peace. Negligence to house or child became my daily choice.

Long after this time in our lives, I came across a book that described most simply the essentials in such an undertaking. It was written by a doctor who specializes in the field of his own affliction: Earl R. Carlson, M.D., *Born That Way*. In it he writes, "The value of muscle training depends upon a number of factors. Before the exercises are started, there should be a preliminary relaxation period. A calm and quiet atmosphere is essential, and the teacher should be a person with a temperament and a personality conducive to relaxation. With younger children it is necessary to assist them passively until they are able to carry out the movements by themselves. Spasticity is a stiffness of movement. The limb moves as a solid piece; this condition is spoken of as a clasp-knife rigidity because if the muscle is moved by another person, a certain degree of resistence is encountered, which is intense at first, then diminishes rapidly as the range of movement increases." Through all my experimenting with our own daughter, I had learned this.

It became necessary to devise means of breaking down lengthier chores so that I might still accomplish things after Patty's therapy. I did shorter but more frequent laundries. With casseroles and stews I could depend on reheats when I returned so late from the city each time. I did my ironing in spurts. And if Arthur dreamed of luscious apple pies and frosted three-layer cakes, he had to settle for those lifted from the delicatessen's shelf.

46

Together we were learning, Arthur and I, to accept with good humor that which we could not have or do in order to meet the added responsibilities. What pained us most was watching Patty crawl month after month after month, her knees bruising despite the extra pads I had sewed into her coveralls. For as she crawled the pants' legs rode up and the padded area lost its place. We were unable to confine her travel in her ambitions to be with the other children. Her knees were now becoming infected from the rough spots she continuously crawled over. I wanted to weep each time I bathed her knees with antiseptic solution.

When we felt so defeated, Patty's own sweet tolerance was our major source of courage.

Gail's compassion for her sister became more and more evident. Since I had always kept watch on Patty from my window unnoticed, I never gave Gail the entire responsibility of her care. Whatever help she wished to give would come voluntarily.

How my heart quickened the afternoon she excused herself from her playmates who were going off to further points venturing into more exciting play. Gail said to them, "Well, I have to go now; Patty is all alone."

For the summer afternoons cousins Louie and Craig came to play down in the cleared grounds. Gail climbed the graduated drive to come after Patty to make sure that she missed none of it. They played a mild game (Gail saw to that, too) of Cowboys and Indians, giving Patty an Indian headpiece and marking her slim little chest and forearms with red candy-coated jaw-teasers. Although none of Patty's movements were standing, I observed contented absorption in the game. As I watched Gail's gentle, loving patience, I hoped that as she grew nothing would discourage such pleasing grace.

By now, a part of the therapy practice was to walk behind Patty, bending over her while she grasped my index fingers in walking guidance. Her fear of falling prohibited her relaxation, and it required a great deal of coaxing before she would give even the least cooperation. With my legs very close to hers, she offered a try, but her whole body remained rigid. So it was slow work. If she relaxed for only a few steps, it was rewarding.

One of our morning exercises was standing her against the walls, heels touching the baseboard for balance. For this I sat on the floor immediately in front of her, concealing whatever frustration I felt, and beckoned her softly to leave that wall. She was too frightened! She would tense her hands against the wall which offered her safety. After many weeks I noticed her growing desire to leave it as I invited. *"Today* you can make it, Patty." I truly felt she might. Something inside her told her, "No."

At that time no long-sleeve coveralls were sold for the creeping age. I designed one for Patty's warmth and cleanliness. As fast as she wore out the knees I added new patches.

Such work led me never to close my sewing machine. It was a busy implement without the coverall patching, as I tried to keep our clothes in shape, to lengthen their service, and to build a school wardrobe for Gail.

Our bonds had all been cashed (ones accumulated from Arthur's salary deductions) to pay fuel costs. On occasion we accepted a five or ten dollar loan from Mother, but it made us uneasy knowing how long it took to repay even such small amounts.

From so much crawling, Patty's shoes also demanded constant attention. It was necessary to purchase two

48

pair at a time and they had to be good ones. The uppers would begin to scuff after a week and start to tear through the quality leather. The very tip of the soles would wear down as quickly as the toe uppers. Finally, our cobbler devised a scheme; he glued a soft piece of leather over the scuffed portion and at the same time repaired only the far front of the soles. In ten days or two weeks, I would be back with another pair. With wings, the shoes could have reached their destination without me.

Late on one June evening, sitting in the glider together, listening to the frogs and whippoorwill and watching the passing traffic bound for the open-air theater two miles up, Arthur lamented, "We'll be married ten years next week, won't we?"

"Yep. We sure got ourselves involved, didn't we?" I quipped.

"What d'ya say, we go out and celebrate?"

"Can we afford it?" I challenged.

"Have we been able to afford *anything* that's been happening to us? It happened just the same. This might be just what we need after all this." He could stop there. I was sold.

The morning of our anniversary, Arthur handed me a bill. "I've been saving some green stuff. I want you to go downtown and buy a dress. Something special." I winced knowing full well how he had figured to save this much.

With misgivings for using the money for such a vain cause, I nevertheless melted when I saw the pale pink linen with grey briar sweeping the entire circular skirt of the dress. With it wrapped and paid for, I was on the next bus home.

My vanity had taken a back seat with all that Patty required. My hair had been as simply kept as civilized living permitted. Blouses and skirts were all I wore.

49

With suspense, Gail watched the transformation from deluged mother to dated wife. She whispered something to her daddy which started them both laughing.

Arthur and I felt very lighthearted as we sauntered out to the car. The children were in good hands and Patty herself was asleep and well. The evening was a tonic for both of us at the dine-and-dance eighteen miles north.

The next day brought us back to problems at hand.

*P*atty outgrew the standard sizes in white knee socks with elastic tops which helped prevent infection to her reddened knees. I combed the children's speciality shops without success. I then returned to the store from which I had been purchasing them up to now and explained our necessity. The sales clerk spoke with the store manager and a special order was arranged.

It was not the first time store clerks went out of their way to please in Patty's behalf. Of course it required my description of the problem, and I did often feel uneasy about the need to do so to these strangers. But these downtown "strangers" turned out to be exceedingly thoughtful people who to this day never fail to inquire about our daughter's welfare.

There was one thing we were unable to find a solution for—slippering of Patty's feet. It would have added to her comfort in the morning to wear slippers before the shoes went on. With her tight heel cords, her heels failed to touch the ground. Any slippers bought for her would fall right off. Too, the feet were pathetically skinny.

Another thing to puzzle us was that while she seemed bright and interested in familiar, homey things, she took no notice of a bird on the clothesline or a squirrel in the backyard or a plane in the sky. Why? We kept trying to figure that out.

We began taking Sunday afternoon rides up to the Lakes Region, bringing along picnic lunches. We deliberately planned our spots next to farmland on the way so that she would "take in" the cows, horses, sheep which customarily intrigue little children.

She exhibited no response.

Gail herself wanted to share the delight with Patty. Patty was just not interested. So, one Tuesday I broached the question to Patty's speech therapist, although I was afraid what the answer might be.

Not in the least surprised, Mr. Clem said, "Short interest span."

"Is that what it is? Is it permanent? Can it be broadened?" I asked cautiously, feeling very much like my older child who felt certain to receive a negative answer when what she hoped for was a "yes."

"Yes," he replied. "Repetition of the things she seems not interested in will eventually make her curious."

Turning to Patty invitingly, "Shall we hear what our voice sounds like on the tape recorder, Patty?" As I watched him interest her in the tools he used, I saw how easily he gained a child's confidence with almost no effort at all.

In further visits there I noticed older children, some who suffered maladjustment in school, often confide in him their embarrassments over their speech impediments. We learned that Patty had a number of fears that added further to her affliction. She was terrified by the noise of a hair dryer, vacuum cleaner, or any kind of blower. The fire alarm, unfortunately close to our neighborhood was the worst of all. Excitement was only one of the things that could bring on a convulsion, the other being indigestion, fatigue, or the onset of an illness. Wherever we went, Arthur or I carried a small bottle of phenobarbitol. For those occasions that held extra excitement, we rested Patty's nerves with the sedative. So that she would not fall dependent on such medication, we tried to always avoid the causes, lessening the need.

A reasonable length of time elapsed and I worried about Patty-Anne's growing lack of interest in her exercises and her resistance to "going soft," an absolute must before one can begin the therapy. I discussed the difficulty with Dr. J at the clinic. He suggested radio music as a possibility. Two months later, I reported to him that the music was so varied in tempo that it only excited her, and I would lose whatever I gained in the previous minutes. He asked if we owned a record player. I told him we didn't. "Well, get one and find suitable music." His attitude was to stop at nothing for these little patients.

Just before we made the rounds looking for a not-too-expensive player, the three little dark-eyed boys next door told their mother, "Mommy, why don't we bring ours over to Patty?" These generous little fellows insisted, "Honest, Mrs. StCyr, we don't need it, we don't need it." There was spontaneous joy in their lending. Patty's affliction had worked deep into these children. While we practiced gait-training outside, I often noticed them stop their play to study her progress. They were concerned for their young neighbor, and they rejoiced over her improvements.

The record player, being a "78" without automatic changer, did not allow for me to continue through one whole exercise number before the record finished. I explained this carefully to the boys after several days, and they understood. We all thanked them for their generosity and thoughtfulness.

We found an "arc" of a combination player which had been used as a trade-in for a television set at one of the shops. It was huge, but if there was one thing we had lots of, it was space. Size was not important. Performance was.

As the men delivered it, I watched compassion cross their faces when they saw our crawling Patty. I was very grateful for our new investment. It gave me just what I needed. I had found four records of three-quarter time music. The few mornings I lost the argument to the dishes, Patty would crawl out to me, begging "Ma ma, my la la." Then I could hardly dry my hands fast enough. The music had a soothing effect. Patty went plenty soft as I worked the legs, the feet, the heel cords, then our practice roll on the rug, to the right, then to the left. As the records began to wear out, we returned to buy a second one, of the same title. And when the "arc" breathed its last, we decided to buy a new longer-lasting model which would serve the whole family and be a nice piece of furniture for the living room.

In attempts to cultivate her interest in animals, I bought only the simplest of picture books. Working with Patty on these books, I again had cause to wonder; she never pointed out an interesting picture or became excited as I read and re-read the nursery rhymes. During this time doubt filled the air, and my courage needed refueling. I tried to remember the story of Marie Curie who continued stirring the pots of pitchblende in which she and her husband Pierre suspected radium existed. It was long and tedious work. They worked for the benefit of science; our concentration was to help one single, presently helpless human being.

Chapter 6

*P*atty was close to four years when Ray and Betty Chicoine moved into the small white cottage next to ours. Their tiny, beautiful twenty-months-old daughter became Patty's companion. Her parents became our fast friends.

At the end of Patty's morning exercises, Betty would have her pot of tea ready, alongside the children's milk and graham crackers. Sipping the tea, we were given excellent opportunity to watch these two girls at play.

Gail was outside with Cousin Lou during the summer days, and attended school the rest of the time.

Betty always kept little Daune's toys in the lower drawer beneath the red maple cabinets. Once Patty arrived, Betty would spill all the toys in front of the children. When one appealed to Patty, she picked it up.

Daune, who was just going through the "that's-mine-let-me-have-it" stage, would also become attracted to it and claim it. The process would repeat itself. Without sufficient opposition, it was easy victory for Daune. Betty would rise and reclaim it for my daughter, giving Lesson Number One in sharing to her little girl. I wanted to object; Patty would need many lessons in self-defense and experiences like these would have to serve as the teacher. It wasn't hard for me to recall Gail's having gone through the possessive stage with strange playmates when she was Daune's age.

As soon as I was able to visit with Betty alone, I explained how fast Patty was approaching school age and how we would not want her unable to protect herself or to get the feeling that other children wanted to take advantage of her. It frightened me that she might ever feel intentionally hurt. Daune was only a toddler—if only her behavior would force Patty out of her easy submission to show a little fight!

No, Betty couldn't see it. Patty was handicapped; Daune had everything as the challenger. As the conversation ended, Betty was misty-eyed with sympathy for Patty and she walked away unable to finish speaking her thoughts.

Then there was my brother John. His son Craig was a typical Jack-be-nimble-Jack-be-quick whose hazel eyes sparkled. He could no more walk slowly than Patty could walk—period! So when John visited us with his wife and son, John would break out in a cold sweat as he watched his son racing through the rooms while Patty crawled. Exercising self-restraint, Arthur and I would call the necessary whoa's, noticing Patty wince while she edged out of Craig's path.

While Arthur felt exceedingly tender toward Patty, he would be the last to discourage her independence. Neither of us felt that her confidence-building could wait until she was off walking, if ever she would walk.

We always remained close-by for these experiences and carefully studied the children who would present them. Consequently it wasn't long before we noticed Patty adopting a strategy. While she loitered, she studied Craig's maneuvers, with a wistful look, desiring to copy him. Knowing he was speedy, she learned to wait for him to lead, then began to follow his every turn, under the table and out, circling the chairs, then over the threshholds and on to other rooms.

Not long after that, John settled back—his eyes were misty—witnessing the game in our kitchen, realizing fully the contribution his son had made.

Two years had passed since therapies started. There were still no signs of Patty's walking. I was beginning to question if any of my effort was helping, particularly in the stretching of the heel cord. Every morning except Saturday when I house-cleaned and Sunday when we attended church, I worked with her from nine to almost ten o'clock on physio and the next hour on occupational and speech therapies. Patty was still crawling the balance of the day! I wondered a little more each day what sense it made. I was growing tired. Wasn't there some other kind of help to expedite the walking, *somewhere*?

We prayed, Arthur and I, until each night found us kneeling for longer periods. Pretty soon, for me, words were reduced to two, "Please God, please . . . please!"

Then one day at the clinic I asked Dr. J if he thought braces might give those legs the necessary support. He shook his head negatively.

"Well, then, can you tell us when our child might walk?"

"No, Mrs. StCyr, no one can tell you that."

So no one could tell us that! As Patty's father and mother we had to face the grim possibilities. Suppose she crawled until she were eight, ten, twelve, or suppose for *always*? Crawling children do not go to school.

If crawling were the only reason she might not be able to go to school, then was there someone, somewhere who would approve braces? The legs were so frail-looking. Did they lack the strength to hold her up? What was she afraid of or was she afraid? If she didn't begin to walk early enough would she become so reconciled to it that she would make no further attempt?

Arthur and I decided it would certainly not hurt to receive the opinion of another orthopedic specialist. There was another highly-qualified man in the city whom we had heard a lot about, Dr. Edward Hagerty. I called him. We could see him in three weeks. Our hopes raised.

The day of the appointment I was excited. He reviewed the exercises I was doing on Patty and had us demonstrate her gait-training maneuvers. Then he worked her limbs.

I told him why I came to him. Specifically regarding bracing. Matter-of-factly in his deep voice he said, "No, I wouldn't brace her; I would, however, prescribe forefoot shoes to eliminate the crossing of her feet. No, I couldn't tell you how soon she will be walking."

I waited for him to write out the prescription for the shoes. At least it was a move.

We reached the Boston, Massachusetts Shoe Store we were directed to several days later. My sister Eleanor met us at the terminal and gave the waiting cab driver the address written on the prescription blank.

After measuring Patty's feet, the man told me that the shoes would be ordered from New York and that I would receive them in the mail in a couple of weeks. Eleanor took us to lunch close by, then hailed a cab to take us to her apartment on the Fenway which she shared with another single girl. In all that the last few years involved, I had not had time to see the place. The apartment was spacious and cozy. I mused as I noticed the bright colors on the walls. Eleanor was conservative and I could hardly wait to meet the roommate with such flair. Yellow, chelsea blue and a bit of Chinese decor! Dottie was her name and she was just what the color psychologists would predict. Gay, friendly and fun-loving. She and Patty were immediately drawn to one another. She had little fluffy teddy bears and plastic novelties hidden away in the nightstands beside the beds. The way she insisted on piling Patty's plate at meal time, one would think our daughter had spent a day at hard labor.

During the visits that followed Patty was so excited that she ate very little although her first words to Dottie were, "Eat, Eat!" Eleanor was very familiar with Patty's delicate appetite but she and I were ignored as Dottie heaped on the servings.

Sometime after our first Boston visit the shoes arrived by mail within the date promised. They were handsome sturdy high brown shoes. The toes on each directed outward. They were marked "left" and "right" to avoid mistake when putting them on. They looked very much like a right shoe going on a left foot and vice versa. They cost twelve and one-half dollars. Without a doubt they would offer excellent support for her ankles.

Unaccustomed to immediate results from any action taken in Patty's behalf, we waited patiently for this new investment to pay dividend. I continued with the exercises and gait training.

By now, Betty next door consented to resist interfering in the toy-snatching contest between Daune and Patty. We noticed that Patty would frown when Daune would claim each object. Like any slow game we watched for even the slightest sign of interesting action. The frown might indicate something.

A new practice was added to Patty's physio program. That of rising from a stool. She disliked this practice intensely. It was difficult to train her in it. The stool was made to specifications, ideal for positioning her legs straight together and encouraging correct posture. As instructed by Miss Stanton, I supported her hip with my left hand and pushed back the bent knees gently with my right. I would offer the suggestion for her ascension from the stool. Lacking the confidence, she let her disagreement be known. All the while, soft three-quarter time music played in the background. I made only brief attempts at it, once each day. In this way, she would eventually become receptive to the practice as she had to the others. In these daily encounters, I was learning several subtle approaches until Patty began to enjoy them.

It was in church that we first reaped the reward of that particular effort. We had been taking Patty with us since she was three years old, trying to offer her as many social experiences of the normal child as was humanly possible. Patty would sit passively throughout the Mass. We could be sure that she wouldn't stir off the seat because she was unable to get off or onto a chair unassisted. Arthur, Gail and I were ready to genuflect when we noticed Patty begin to wiggle in her seat. We had learned some time ago to restrain ourselves each time we observed any new attempt on her part. We struggled for composure as we watched her from the corner of our eye—she was lifting her little bottom off the bench. She succeeded in reaching the kneeler independently!

Did we follow the rest of the Mass? How *could* we?

*P*atty wore the forefoot shoes for several months but since she was not yet walking, they remedied nothing. We were unable to determine any benefit from the walking practice since she made no effort whatsoever to move except when I supported her entire body. The longer her legs grew, the thinner they seemed. Her baby legs had proportion. These were spindly.

We felt strongly what we read in Dr. Carlson's book: "If walking is delayed too long, it will become a more difficult matter than if it is acquired during the period of development when the center of balance is constantly changing with growth."

Patty had now passed her fourth birthday and it had become even more painful for us to watch her crawl. Especially since we had given attention to everything that should have promoted her walking. Faith is needed in large quantities. It is frightening not to be able to measure one's reserve.

After Arthur and I discussed the dismal outlook, I wrote to Boston Children's Hospital requesting an appointment. If braces were not advocated there, it was possible that we were wrong.

Promptly the hospital communicated, suggesting we secure a case history from our doctor. They in turn would grant a consultation.

I walked into Dr. J's office somewhat leary of his reaction to this step. How I wished Arthur could be with me at times like these! But his prayers were my strength. He had to make our living. His absence was unavoidable.

I explained the purpose of my visit to Dr. J and frankly expressed our fears for Patty's future. Quietly he sat down in front of his typewriter and wrote up a conscientious report, folded it and addressed its envelope. I was regretting our need to go beyond this doctor's sanction. He was generous enough to offer his genuine good wishes.

Dr. J's letter was off in the mail and I settled back to my routine. Patty spent a little bit of time every day with her friend Daune, crawling as fast as Daune walked.

One day, restless for the letter which would offer new hope, I figuratively turned in my rain check for the cup of tea I had lately forgone in order to catch up on my work at home.

Betty and I cast occasional glances in the children's direction. Patty was picking up a little cardboard horn covered in attractive striped foil. It was shiny, appealing. Little Daune then became interested in it. She threw out her right arm to retrieve it. It required so little effort to win over Patty. All but Patty realized that! Expecting the usual to ensue, Betty and I continued our chat. But within seconds we were stopped short by what was happening beyond the archway. Patty was fighting for her rights! She was pulling and tugging with all her spastic strength and Daune's eyes, that rich heavenly blue, took on a look of bewildering shock. Her jaw dropped as she studied Patty's opposition in refusing to give up the treasured horn.

For how long Betty and I sat there mute as fish, neither of us can remember. But we are sure that of the four of us, Patty at that moment wore the only intelligent expression! Briney tears threatened to alter the flavor of our tea cooling before us. Betty didn't care. She let hers fall. She hadn't believed this ever could happen. From then on it was always fair and square between Daune and Patty.

The letter from the Boston Medical Center arrived with an appointment for March twenty-third. Arthur and I talked of little else.

The days just couldn't pass quickly enough.

Our bag packed (we would stay overnight at Eleanor's apartment before tackling the visit to the hospital), Patty and I were at last seated very happily on the Boston-bound bus. She fell asleep before we reached the halfway mark, and I woke her with difficulty at Park Square where Eleanor waited for us. We reached the apartment by cab in no time at all.

Dottie was just letting herself into the apartment, her arms overladen with groceries. Eleanor started the meal preparation while Dottie greeted Patty. As I freshened up I overheard plans going on for playtime in the park across the way. Dinner over, all four of us walked leisurely over into the playground across the boulevard. I was thinking how this diverting frolic would help her to remember Boston in a pleasanter vein.

We sat on the park bench until Dottie thought it time for Patty to have a ride on the slide. Explaining that Patty had never ridden on a slide before, I listened to the lighthearted comeback, "Well, I haven't either, that is for at least twelve or fourteen years!" Off she sped with our little girl in her arms, Eleanor and I after her. Eleanor waited at the foot of the slide, while I stood at the side. They were having fun, Patty locked in Dottie's arms as they rode down each time, and Eleanor catching them. Patty kept repeating, "More, more."

The next morning, we awoke rested. The girls were off to their offices, I dressed Patty for our trip to the hospital. Anxieties over what to expect occupied my

63

thoughts. I would very soon be hearing what was really best for our daughter. It just might not at all coincide with our own personal opinion. I suppose going into a metropolitan hospital renders all of us timid to one degree or another.

Dropping Eleanor's spare key into my handbag, I walked down the steps of the apartment house to the curb with Patty to await a passing unoccupied cab. That early in the day, I soon saw, such a thing is a rare commodity. And I was not accustomed to the hurrying mass.

I waited almost twenty-five minutes, unable to hail any of the cabs. I mustered up some of my waning courage and told Patty that she and I belonged back in the country. Here on Boylston Street until traffic thinned out, we wouldn't stand a chance. If we dared step out, we would surely be erased from the population figure.

Finally, we caught the eye of a fare-hungry operator, driving more slowly than the others. Relieved, I sunk back in the rear seat, gasping, "Three Hundred Longwood Avenue. Medical Center, please." It had been a long time holding Patty there on the sidewalk, switching from arm to arm.

I commented on the weather to divert Patty's mind in the event that she too was becoming apprehensive. The driver reciprocated and we managed light conversation for the entire distance. He carried Patty to the hospital entrance for me once the fare was settled.

I presented our admittance card at the desk, paid the charge, and learned directions to the Orthopedic Department upstairs. Inside the door labelled ORTHO-PEDICS, we sat until the appointed time. The reception room was gay with all kinds of games and picture books upon little tables for restless young patients.

Two metal cribs were made up in the back of the room for tinier babies to be changed or placed for their bottles. Teenaged aides were present to supervise play among the youngsters.

Patty grew very uneasy as she watched uniformed nurses walking back and forth. Young surgical patients were wheeled through in casts or with crutches laying beside them as they were taken in to one doctor after another for observation. Patty began to whimper pessimistically. To change her mood, I walked further back to where other children played. Her attention was sufficiently held until the nurse called our name and led us into one of the empty rooms to await the doctor whose name was on our appointment card.

When he came in, announcing his name, he reviewed Patty's case history from the folder he carried with him. He then looked up at us. To me, he said, "Now Mrs. StCyr, will you tell us just exactly what brought you to us. As thoroughly as you can."

I felt shivers up and down my back. Again, I wished I could have Arthur with me. These were far from easy times, meeting the all-knowing professional people, having them study your countenance while hearing your maternal rendition, never once relieving you with even a brief response. We had waited for this day so impatiently that I couldn't afford to stammer or forget.

I waited several seconds before I was able to begin. I decided to tell him of our many fears. I described the practices we engaged in daily, how Patty reacted to them, the things from which we saw no concrete results. I confessed our theory on the heel cord situation concerning prolonged crawling. Did it not reduce all benefit of my work of over two years? Wouldn't braces rectify this disturbing, unjust score? This was what brought me here.

"O.K." he said, "Let's take the shoes off and the slacks and jersey. We will take a look-see."

Ungraciously, Patty submitted to the examination.

Then the doctor asked me to go through some of our exercises. He advised me to keep Patty unclothed while he brought in another doctor whose name he courteously mentioned. Butterflies raced through my stomach. While I waited I tried to look relaxed, for my daughter's sake. She too studied my countenance!

The older man was a specialist in brain-damaged cases. Other mothers back home had mentioned his outstanding reputation. He examined, then asked Patty to slap his hand. She, misconstruing his motive, became frightened and refused to cooperate. I became flustered. But the senior doctor acted well-used to this behavior. "That's all. You may dress her now."

The terms the two men exchanged did not seem so foreign to me anymore. They were ones I'd heard over and over again throughout Patty's rehabilitation.

Withdrawing a cellophane-wrapped red lollipop from the pocket of his white frock and handing it to Patty, the young doctor asked us to wait here until he returned. Patty sat relaxed, enjoying her lollipop.

After a long time, the doctor was back. He came directly to the point. "Well, Mrs. StCyr, you are going to have your braces." I opened my mouth to voice my pleasure but he went right on. "In view of your own findings as parents and the time you have already devoted, we feel they might be given a try." Again I started to speak. "Now, please understand, Mrs. StCyr, that braces alone will not do the work. You realize that, I hope?"

So very grateful, I explained that I was not looking for something to take over the work for me, but for some aid. "Good, then," he said, "we are glad to be able to help you. Now with my prescription here, you take your baby over to the brace shop across the street from the hospital where she will be measured for short leg braces. When they are completed, we will send you an appointment to come down again." Then he added, "Oh yes, you must purchase new high shoes from your own city and mail them to the shop at your earliest convenience."

I was thrilled. I thanked him and we left. The elevator took us back downstairs where I noticed the hospital cafeteria. While the excitement lessened the importance of food, I felt a taste of soup might be needed to hold us through the measuring of braces. I had no idea whether we might need to wait or just what this measuring involved. We relaxed over our soup and took in the many faces of people coming and going in this busy hospital.

We walked across the street and up the steps to the brace shop. While we waited, I noticed all types of orthopedic appliances for the young and full grown.

When the attendant was ready we were called into an anteroom where the tracing of Patty's legs only required a few minutes. Once over with, we were out on the corner standing again in wait of a cab.

Back in Eleanor's apartment, I slumped into the nearest chair. I expressed my unrestrained joy to my child. "We are going to have braces, Patty. We are going to have braces!" She looked back at me and her eyes gleamed. She was pleased because I was pleased.

After a very light lunch, she had her nap. While she slept, I delved into deep thought. This was Good Friday. New hope was given us.

When Patty awoke, I walked with her in my arms to the nearest church to kneel. We did not hurry.

The day was beautiful, yet people scurried about hardly conscious of it, I thought. Their hurrying made me more aware of the pace to which I personally had been slowed. To allow for the affliction which God had sent us, for all our sakes, we had to lessen the hurry and excitement.

Coming out of church on the way back to the apartment, I swapped Patty from one arm to another. As we reached the apartment entrance, I sat Patty down as I worked the key into the lock. When I stooped to pick her up, my eyes were drawn to her feet. One shoe was missing!

Retracing my steps to the church, I found no sign of the tailored brown shoe. Either children had picked it up or passing feet had kicked it behind bordering hedges.

Sadness accompanied the joy I knew that day. Not so much over the loss of the shoe but over the condition which caused it to drop off unnoticed. The thin little feet with the heel not quite touching bottom. Those short tendons. The lace must have worked loose as I shifted her in my arms.

The lump in my throat gave way to choking sobs once Patty became engrossed with the toys Dottie had left on the divan.

The full meaning of Good Friday, as never before, reached inside me. The tears His own mother had shed witnessing Him crucified!

I bathed my face with cold water and forced myself to think of the hours just ahead. I would be home, relaying good news.

At 7:15 P.M., our bus stopped directly across the road from our cottage. Arthur and Gail shot out of the house to meet us and to carry Patty across.

Arthur made us a light snack, while I did all the talking. Patty was now fully awake and enjoyed being the subject of eager conversation. Arthur then undressed her and said, "Well now I guess that's getting somewhere, isn't it, Patty?"

Chapter 7

*P*ing-pong balls and a doll's miniature clothesline with paper clothes were added to Patty's speech therapy to encourage breath control. We had already begun blowing out birthday candles, using the "puh" sound instead of the usual "whoo" sound. We followed this practice with bubble blowing, attempts at singing, blowing whistles and horns. Now blowing the ping-pong balls off the table fascinated her.

One day while I rinsed my wash, I heard a soft little humming in the hallway. Patty-Anne was sitting on the first step with her dolly in her arms, lullabying her to sleep!

At last, too, Patty became interested in mechanical toys. Although her fingers lacked the coordination to wind them, her eyes would follow their path as they rode along the floor. Gail wound and rewound them for her.

About this same time, Patty's aunt Rose managed to hold Patty's interest sufficiently to have her match the animals on the cards of an Animal Rummy game.

When I returned from town to claim Patty at Rose's, I marvelled at the concentration gained by my sister-in-law who shared our mutual concern for our child's short interest span.

On April 24 we went after our finished braces. Also on this visit, Patty was to have her first psychological testing.

Over dessert, Dottie divulged plans formed between herself and her fiance, Stan. With Eleanor as curious as myself, we were told that she and Stan were going to spend this evening scaring up a stroller for me for the next afternoon's leisure, once we returned from the hospital. As soon as Stan called for Dottie, they left on their thoughtful mission.

Sure enough, in the morning an outmoded wicker stroller waited outside the apartment door, all brushed up and waiting to be put into service. The lines of that stroller told me that in Stan's neighborhood there were no babies younger than himself.

At the hospital the tiny brown leather-covered steel braces stood at attention on the nurse's desk with a tag strung from the buckle labelled "StCyr." I couldn't wait to claim them.

Patty herself was now anxious for them; her daddy had thumbtacked to the kitchen wall a picture of a braced little girl taken from a brochure we had received.

Talking with the doctor as he tried Patty's braces on for the first time, I was unable to hide my appreciation. The doctor smiled warmly but repeated, "You must not discontinue her exercises because of these, Mrs. StCyr." I just nodded my head. I had no intention of eliminating the therapies.

We went on to another section of the hospital to await word from the psychologist that she was ready for us. It took some time. It was eleven o'clock before we were admitted into a room with small tables and shelves housing all types of objects for testing. The psychologist was a pleasant young woman with lots of charm and enthusiasm. She wore a royal-blue frock and wore her hair pinned simply behind her ears.

To create a relaxed atmosphere for her patient, she talked leisurely with the mother for the first few moments, then ever so casually spilled out about twenty miniature objects on the table in front of Patty. They resembled furnishings for little girls' dollhouses. "Please hand me the cup and saucer, Patty." Without delay, Patty had them in her fingers and did as she was bid. "Now the clock please." Patty's eyes quickly spotted the article. She handed it to the woman she so obviously had taken a liking to. "Can you find me the little bed?" With a proud little "Yeah," Patty accommodated. So it went, while I watched thankfully.

Then the psychologist took out a number of plaques holding several different shapes which she slowly scattered across the table-top, asking Patty to fit them into their respective recesses. Patty didn't score on this at all; I hadn't felt she would since the puzzles at home took a great deal of repetition before she realized accomplishment at them.

Any of the toys in which Patty showed insufficient interest were neutrally put aside by the psychologist and new ones offered in their place. Once this testing was complete, she handed Patty a paper and pencil, requesting her to draw a circle. Patty merely pushed the pencil back and forth, managing only stingy, jagged lines.

After the testing was over, the psychologist picked up a picture book along with some interesting toys and asked if Patty would mind waiting outside the room while "Doctor" chats with Mommy. Patty didn't mind. She trusted the lady in the royal-blue frock.

71

"From what we succeeded at, I would score your daughter as eighteen months retarded. She seems very well-adjusted. Enjoys people, doesn't she?" I nodded. "For the present, speech and other accompanying factors limit my testing. Patty's shape and color discrimination is in need of developing."

She wanted to know my husband's and my attitude toward having an afflicted child; if we felt the necessary changes strongly, what our other child's behavior was like in reference to her handicapped sister.

Warmth and sober concern were what we felt. And I gave her examples of Gail's kindness and generosity toward Patty every day.

"Fine. Fine. Now does Patty help you with the housework?" she questioned. I hesitated, puzzled.

"Does Patty help you with the housework?" she asked again, realizing I didn't believe the question. "By that I mean does she show interest to take her hand at Mother's work?"

With restored confidence, I replied, "Oh, well, she has taken my rinse cloth from the basin, as I wash the window panes and rubbed it over the floor."

"Splendid! Marvelous! Encourage it." she exclaimed with sensational appreciation.

If Patty's Dad were only here! Every time, I had cleared away all evidence of our Patty's "helping" before he reached home.

The psychologist was reminded of her next appointment as she got a look at her watch and gently dismissed us. She added how anxious she would be to learn of the improvement in Patty upon her next visit scheduled.

After this, we went straight on to Patty's routine check-up. That completed, we took the elevator to the office where we paid the twenty-four dollars for the leather-covered steel braces.

Back at the apartment I cooked a meal—or tried,

city gas being twice as fast as bottled country gas. I burned the chops and boiled out the peas. Should have bought lunch at the hospital cafeteria, I thought, as I opened the hall door to rid the apartment of the un-savory smells smouldering from its kitchen. I slipped out to the nearby variety store. Two fatal meals like that in the same day could put Eleanor and Dottie on a tenants' black list. When I left the store, I was car-rying old reliable chicken and rice soup and a package of soda crackers. It tasted surprisingly good.

After we freshened up, Patty sat obediently and enthusiastically in the easy chair next to the French doors leading from the kitchen to the living room while I wheeled the stroller the length of the hall and down off the front steps to the street. I then returned to pick up my passenger, locking the apartment after us.

Unlike early morning, traffic was no hindrance to our crossing the boulevard. We strolled leisurely down the paved walk into the green expanse which dropped from the heights of the streets embracing it. To the right we noticed a small boy stirring the serene pond water with his stick as he remained in his crouched position, entranced. The springtime sun focused di-rectly on its young subject.

The trees all about us were just freshly budded, the kind of day that inspires poets—the first day our daughter wore her braces. Watching the little boy I marvelled at his freedom and independence. His mother was nowhere in sight. Would Patty one day enjoy his kind of freedom? This thought recalled the fears, temporarily forgotten in the excitement over the braces. It would be some time before we would know if braces were the answer.

Now we were passing another little fellow digging with his spoon in a tiny hollow of earth in the process

of loading his colorful metal truck. He was too engrossed to notice us, but his mother beside him looked
soulfully toward Patty's legs. "Did she have polio?"
she asked, looking straight up at me. I would be asked
this many times.

"No, Patty was injured at birth." It was necessary to
slow down the stroller. As I resumed my walk, the
woman pursued conversation. "I always pray for my
little fellow here. God sent him to me whole and well,
and I ask all the time that He will help me to keep him
so."

"He looks quite robust; I don't think you need to
worry."

Contradicting, she admonished, "Oh, but we *do!*"

I stopped. She was trying to be friendly. And we
did have time today. Besides, it was such a relief to
have my daughter's weight in the stroller instead of in
my arms.

"All that way!" the woman said when I told her
where we were from. This made me smile. Especially
after the cabdriver telling me he had, only three days
before, driven Minnesota parents with their afflicted
child to the hospital from the Boston airport. Nevertheless, I considered my trip hard enough.

After a few more comments, the woman bade her
reluctant son with his truck and spoon locked under
his arm to "come along." They walked as far as one of
the park exits with us, then Patty and I lingered a
while longer enjoying the leisure.

Once more I packed our overnight bag and jour-
neyed home. When we got there, Patty was as happy
over her new braces as another child might be over
a new bike. She found her enthusiasm matched by
Gail's and Arthur's. It was at times like this that we
were thankful for our first child's normalcy and her
healthy attitude toward her sister.

With the braces, we all thought that perhaps the exercise which would contribute most to Patty's walking might be the one encouraging her to leave the wall. One morning less than two months later, I was to realize success.

Patty *looked* ready, but then she had in the past. "Okay Patty? Right now!" I said. I couldn't afford to lose this moment. Her face was eager. Her eyes looked to mine. Her lips parted but not a sound came from her. She loosened herself from that wall and moved the feet away from the baseboard ever so slowly. She was coming!

One, two, "the other foot, Patty!" (In her trepidation, she was trying to use only one foot.) "This foot now. The other foot." Whoops! Into my arms she fell, giggling nervously. She dared. She *dared*. She didn't walk but for the first time Patty overpowered her fear of falling. That was a giant step in itself.

***

*N*ew words joined her vocabulary: "there, why, here, and hey" (with a strong "h" now). "See" was followed by "tea," and "yeps" in favor of "yeah."

Patty began to address me as "Peg." It tickled me because it was the first word she used which had a "g" at the end. Once she got the real feel with this nickname of mine, she attempted other short words with the same ending.

On our next visit to the rehab center Patty got excited over a black metal doll carriage with an orange and blue clad doll resting comfortably beneath a patchwork quilt. Miss Stanton stood Patty between the carriage and herself, folding Patty's fingers over the carriage handle. Fearing that Miss Stanton planned to leave her there alone, Patty began to cry nervously, losing all interest in the carriage.

Miss Stanton reassured her, "No, Patty, I'm going to push too. We'll go strolling with the baby together." Then Patty became herself again, confidence restored.

She was tense and dragged her feet just as she did at home with me whenever she was not in favor of her gait training. Miss Stanton wasn't hurrying and I couldn't understand why she was allowing Patty so much time with the doll and carriage. Then I noticed her slowly lift her own arms away from the handle. Patty was unaware. The therapist remained behind Patty but she gave no help. When our daughter realized the absence of those extra arms, she stiffened and began to whimper, ready to fall backward. Without a word, Miss Stanton put her arms forward closing her fingers once again beside Patty's while they pushed the buggy into the therapy room. There was a fifteen-pound weight under that patchwork quilt which steadied the carriage. Arthur could shorten the handle of Gail's forgotten carriage up in the storeroom. With our bathroom scale hidden under a little cotton mattress, we would have another instrument for home therapies!

How it lifted our spirits to see her standing upright off that floor for just a bit! We hid the bathroom scale under the doll mattress as planned and practiced the carriage-pushing in the living room where she could take her spills on the rug should she unmindfully lose her grip.

The following Saturday afternoon, just after Arthur came home from work, I walked out to the glider to sit with Patty in my lap. She had been fine all morning but was now whimpering pettishly. Arthur was preparing to go into town to the barbershop. Patty was falling asleep. Then I noticed with alarm that she was in another convulsion! Arthur had never seen her in one.

I made the distance into the kitchen on weak and trembling legs. Arthur, no more calm than I, filled the large deep-white sink and rapidly stripped the table of its linen cloth to place bathmat, towels and crib blanket ready, once the lukewarm bath and sedative would remedy the attack. He brought me ice cubes between wet washcloths for her forehead. I held her in the water up to her shoulders.

"Why to *her*, just why to her?" Arthur kept repeating. "What has she ever done to deserve this?" "God doesn't punish this way. I won't believe it," I said. I was crying in complete helplessness as I drew the washcloth over our unconscious child, again and again, praying all the while that the next moment would bring her back to consciousness.

"But why . . . " he sounded now without faith.

"I don't know *what* to ask anymore, Arthur, but you? Not you. You still *kneel.*"

He didn't answer. He may have stopped hoping, but not praying. How I envied his absorption in prayer while I lay wondering, confused, in mine.

By the time Patty-Anne's seizure was over, Arthur and I were emotionally exhausted. It was some time before color returned to our daughter's cheeks.

*L*ike the calm following the storm, Patty was very well and alert on Sunday. (We discovered the spell was caused by a sectioned orange she ate too soon after her medicines. Patty did not digest as easily as another child might.) In fact, my mother was beginning to think that Patty showed new vitality after these nightmarish attacks. New attempts *were* made within only days afterward. Patty insisted that the parlor blinds be closed while she rocked her baby and fed her. Shortly after, Patty placed her baby down for a pretend nap so that she might investigate my hat box. She tried on each hat (perennials), carefully appraising what it did for her. I was convinced that her personal appearance was one thing she would nurse with pride.

To the amusement of all who knew her, she demonstrated a passionate love for any doll newly received, whether it be a five-inch shelf doll, a seventeen-inch rag doll, or a beauty with magic, vinyl skin and lustrous, saran hair. That it be her newest was all-important. Once she received it, the rest of her little make-believe family never knew so much as a cool goodnight kiss. My sympathy always went out to these forlorn, rejected lovelies, once so spoiled.

One day the spirit moved me to wash my white kitchen range. I became aware that this same spirit had prodded Patty. As I was completing my job, she began to cry until I understood that she wanted me to leave the pan of water.

I gave her a new supply of sudsy water, no more than a pintful. I watched my little apprentice, blissfully ignorant of the merit of system, scrub the baseboard, then the inlaid linoleum of the floor, then the oven door of my stove! Good Lord! Do I have to take this *too?* With nagging misgivings, I retrieved the pan. Arthur didn't work overtime that day and when he walked in I was disappointed to hear his "Peg, what's that smudge on the oven door?" His grey-green eyes showed puzzlement.

"The handle maybe?" I said. My back was turned.

"Well, come out and see." He couldn't believe I knew it was there and would leave such a thing.

"Oh Beautiful! MARvelous!" I exclaimed with all the gusto of a truly gratified psychologist. My arms waved flamboyantly in the air.

"Are you all right, Peg?" He looked worried.

"Can't you recognize a skill in your youngest daughter? She has only *begun*. The psychologist at Children's Hospital tells me this should be encouraged!"

With my joke done, I moved closer to kiss the receding hairline of my tired husband. He saw no humor in his daughter's handicap. Turning to Patty who was hanging onto her swing in the doorway, he picked her up saying to her, "So you've had a busy day cleaning the kitchen?" She answered him with a happy smile and snuggled closer to him.

Off they went into the living room where Daddy read the evening paper. While I remained in the kitchen to broil the meat and wait for Gail to come in and wash up, I thought about Arthur's deep seriousness over Patty. It was indeed pity in every sense of the word. We knew we mustn't allow ourselves pity. But human nature doesn't change easily. It took many years for Arthur to regard her as something like a normal child. And when I first noticed it happening I felt such great relief. He, Gail and Patty were busy at something in an adjoining room and I overheard him saying crossly, "What's the matter, are you a cripple? You do it." He was addressing his afflicted daughter. I realized that he no longer felt pity—love, but no pity.

Chapter 8

*T*his year, Christmas came without snow. We noticed a new exhilaration in Patty over the tinselled tree. We found her several times tugging at the packages accumulating there for small cousins. Her own and Gail's were always hidden until after they were fast asleep on Christmas eve.

Things for Gail were always so easy to find. This year, among other things for Patty, I found a miniature mailbox in which were five variously shaped holes into which colored blocks fitted. Each block was a different color. This would improve her shape and color discrimination.

Following the holidays, a little paint set that one of her cousins gave her interested her most. Soon to follow was her fascination with ladies' handbags. Desiring to be smart and fashionable, she was next caught nonchalantly holding a pencil between her fingers, then placing it between her lips, withdrawing it, and sending out the invisible smoke, actually flicking the imaginary ashes into the nearby ashtray! Did I think our daughters wouldn't smoke just because I personally chose not to? I told Patty that I hoped her daddy wouldn't mind her new habit. She withdrew the pencil with embarrassment. This was the first time I ever noticed embarrassment in her. It was good.

After school and on weekends, Gail was allowed to wander a little further from home. She was now eight years old and extremely reliable.

Patty cried each time she saw her sister leave. I would tell her that Gail needed to play with girls her age and that none lived close enough to our house. For incentive, I added, "When you can walk, maybe Gail will ask you along."

Came the day I heard her knock on the window at Gail with her companion outside and saucily utter, "Ha, Ha!" as she wrinkled up her nose in an "I don't care" attitude.

Who could know what she really felt? Was it: "I can't walk like all of you, but I don't care"—all the while wishing it weren't so important to her?

It was about this time that Arthur was admitted to the hospital for his tonsillectomy. His throat had been irritating him for some time and he had hoped it might subside. When it didn't, he made the decision to have it over with once and for all. It made Gail feel quite experienced, having gone through the ordeal before either of her parents. She was in second grade now, doing very well in school, and she made friends easily. Her dad was indeed proud of his blonde Gail.

Patty-Anne, beside her, was such a contrast. When she passed her fourth birthday and wasn't walking although she was crawling at a remarkable speed, I began to wonder if the only way she would ever navigate would be on her hands and knees. The increasing physical growth only made the crawling a sad sight.

Without a doubt, the exercises had made her more

limber. She was talking a little, although very little. Her speech was indistinct. When she couldn't make herself understood, she motioned, and we in the house understood.

She displayed a glowing personality.

But, oh God, how long can I bear seeing her continue to crawl? How will she go to school? How will she compete and socialize with her generation? She cannot stand; she topples like a chair with one of its legs broken.

If I collapse, unable to continue the therapies, how far will she go?

God, do you hear me? You do not answer me.

I was handling my rosary. I was going through the motions of my Catholic faith, but I came face to face with a truth; I had stopped believing. Yet, I hoped someone would hear my unrecited prayer. My fingers moved over the beads. My lips would not cooperate.

Then I reached my darkest day.

We had just had lunch, Patty-Anne and I. Gail was in school. Daddy was at work. As always, she was smiling sweetly at me, trustingly. She could feed herself. How grateful I was for that!

But I am weary, I feel alone. I am no longer optimistic. I cannot go on without my faith. It was what had buoyed me up right along.

I washed my baby's face. Yes, she was a baby, innocent and helpless.

Hugging her closer to me, I brought her upstairs to her crib. I removed her braces, the thing we'd hoped would accomplish her walking. I kissed her and put the coverlet over her. Then drew the blinds to darken the room.

My chin was quivering as I closed her door. I leaned against it, hoping to hold back the flood of tears pressing over the last weeks, days, hours, minutes.

As I reached the foot of the stairs, I bent over the Victorian newel-post and I let myself cry.

Then I decided once more to try to contact God. Not like all the other times when I whispered quietly and reverently, but in choking sobs, I asked Him how He could have chosen *me* to serve this child? I had reached my limit. I was not capable. With all His wisdom, why had He not chosen someone more stalwart.

I had tried. I had failed. Now, what becomes of my child?

No consolation came.

It was to Betty next door that I admitted my despair. Betty had a quality rare in even the oldest and most solid friendships; she wasn't smug. Her Christianity would not tolerate smugness.

By mere instinct, Betty felt the depth of my sorrow. She said that she believed it was fatigue and stress which accounted for my grim outlook, that her own faith might wane under similar strain. "My faith has never been tested," she said softly.

It was close to midnight when I returned home from our talk that night. Her husband was away on one of the out-of-state trips necessary to his work.

I hadn't wished Arthur or my family to know the full extent of my discouragement. They all worried as it was.

Then I began, as had Arthur, to pity Patty-Anne, listing mentally the insurmountable obstacles facing her in life.

It was a walk in the woods that would show me the way; nature has her own way of teaching.

It was the month of May—not always warm, but promising. I had been wondering where next to turn. I had already consulted a priest but his condensed message wasn't practical enough to restore courage in one whose faith had reached its lowest.

Patty-Anne was with my mother for the afternoon.

Although I was convinced that the harmonious endeavor of bird and breeze would be wasted on me that day, I started into the woods which were so close to our home. I walked on and on.

Treading over the brown leaves, decayed and accumulated over the years, I tried to feel some of the exhilaration which this had afforded me every other year. But my pessimism only heightened as I viewed the barren stretch before me where Public Utilities had savagely stripped all its trees in order to extend service to neighboring communities.

These woods didn't belong to me. Yet, I felt they were mine, I had tramped through here often enough, many times bringing both my daughters for whatever they could gain from it. Here had been a natural habitat for the rare species of wildflower. Wild game had claimed sanctuary here. A luxurious bed of purple violets such as I'd never seen elsewhere once blossomed to my left. Maidenfern grew to my right. Lady slippers just ahead of me. What a bleak terrain it was now! It made me cross, as the dead twigs snapped underfoot. Were they echoing my sentiments? Suffering the loss of shade provided by trees, the moist patches had all dried up. No flowers would grow here. How could they? And what about those colorful birds I had seen only here? They would find new refuge, I supposed.

I began hunting for even the barest trace of a wild plant ordinarily due at this time. Not seeing any, I decided to give up and head in another direction for denser woods. Then something *caught* my eye; the unmistakable Jack-in-the-Pulpit. A trio of them! Something in me wanted to rejoice. I stooped curiously to study the soil in which they rallied. It was fast drying up under the sun. Broken twigs and ruthlessly sliced logs lay all about, a trunk remained here and there.

In this uncomplimentary setting, one plant, its growth discouraged by man, adjusted to participate in the spring array with which Nature accommodates her subscribers. I smiled genuinely for the first time in months.

While two of the pulpits rested on tall straight stems, the third had to detour its climb because of a mighty birch log overhead. The stem had been peculiarly twisted during the process of meeting its challenge to blossom equally as beautifully as its companions.

Lingering, I reflected that our daughter, with her defective limbs, would enjoy a participation, however unique it might have to be.

The next day I went at the therapies with renewed vigor and even enthusiasm.

Nature, in the image of God, had just lifted the barrier that had so threateningly been choking off my faith.

*L*eaning over my daughter with her fists closed over my forefingers as we practiced reciprocal motion in walking, I found it not quite so laborious. She became less spastic as the days grew into weeks.

When Gail's friends were present and play ensued outside near the house, Patty was included (Gail refused to overlook her). Patty was gaining courage by hanging onto Gail's two fingers.

The warmer temperatures found her outside more than in. Daune came over more regularly and other children gathered closer to our porch after school hours and on Saturdays. We were making plans for painting our kitchen as soon as doors could be left ajar for longer periods. Mornings were still spent at therapies with bi-weekly trips into the Center.

The windows were only slightly raised with slats of the blinds open wide to welcome the late spring sun. It was the time of year we became impatient to pack away the winter clothes. I was in the middle of doing just that between checks on our handicapped child outdoors. I tried not to have her notice my doing so.

Gail and her friends were jumping rope. The boys were playing marbles and admiring a new gun holster that rested on a broad hip of one of the lads. They were all over on the walk of the next house. I watched Gail glance in Patty's direction. Her next impulse was to bring Patty who was standing against our own porch rail, over to be with the large group.

She walked toward her younger sister in the usual preoccupied manner of any eight-year-old, acting quite grown-up by the time she reached her.

I remained behind the drape as she casually began conversation with the younger one in our family.

Little sister looked up appealingly soliciting, "Daya?" (as she was now calling Gail), extending her left hand for assistance. Gail looked down at the outstretched hand of her sister and withdrew speculatively. I stood immobile, feeling a suspense. What did Gail have in mind? It was not like her to provoke Patty. She never had.

With a tilt of her head, she said, "Well, you can walk now, you know."

My heart started hammering. I looked in the direction of the group of children. They were too entertained to be watching where there was no game. Not to miss any promising sequence, my eyes quickly returned to my own two.

Patty, unmoved by the rejection, returned the treatment matter-of-factly, "OH!" she said and decided she'd be on her way without any further to-do. Taking her right hand away from the porch baluster, she began. It was all happening so swiftly. No inkling. Four birthdays had passed. We had prayed that each next birthday might—and here today, now, she was walking, walking, walking, shoulders back, hands thoughtfully being brought downward as instructed in her therapies. She was controlling her buttocks, mentally calling them to attention so that her walk would be right. Her knees responded to the command of her brain. She was doing her own ordering. The value of posture in walking *had* penetrated effectively! She *had* learned every step of importance. And she made the whole nine yards without falling once!

My tears were falling extravagantly and without shame. They did not, they *could* not, obliterate the vision before me. Patty reached her goal, the children.

Gail was the more excited of the two. She ran to me recklessly allowing the screen door to slam behind her and her eyes were full to the brim. "Oh Mom did you see it? Did you see it?" My eyes spoke for me as I hugged her tightly.

We carried Patty to her Grammy's house to spread the news, then to Rose's. My father was no longer living, but how he would have rejoiced! Gail ran over to tell Betty. Arthur was overjoyed. Everything on that day's agenda was cancelled while we made holiday. We never wanted to forget this day.

Chapter 9

I had been taking Patty into town to acquaint her with the business of shopping. Although she had shown no signs of knowing what money achieves, as we stepped aboard the bus, Grammy put change into the tiny fists.

We took time out for tea at the confectionary store; Patty's tea was a coke. The stop offered a rest.

When I had gained confidence, I sat Patty opposite me in a single booth rather than by my side to teach her social behavior as well as to bolster her ego.

One particularly hot day the booths were quite filled so that we had to sit at the fountain. When we weren't served after quite a wait, Patty's social behavior began to show. She tapped the marble counter with her nickel and said loudly, "Coke! Coke!" No stranger could know how gratifying was this little display.

A few trips after that she pointed to men's shaving lotion in the sundries department exclaiming,

"Daddy, Daddy's," and try as I might to get her away from the department of ladies' handbags, she wouldn't move. I was obliged to explain to the saleswoman that I did not wish to be helped; this was my daughter's pet weakness.

On the street Patty and I walked hand in hand. If she came close to falling it would be more of a topple. I could prevent the fall. She could not walk far. From experience, I learned that if she looked as though she were going to fall, I could save it from happening by bracing her foot with my own foot and by halting long enough for her to regain her balance.

To help her graduate from her infant pattern of walking (always leading with the same foot), I learned that preoccupation was the answer. One day when we reached the center of town after therapy with forty minutes on our hands before the B&M bus was due, I brought Patty into F. W. Woolworth's where we could see the new remodeled departments. She resented my carrying her up the stairs and let me know it. I put her down, strongly reminded of her growing independence. She was showing delight over the variety of counters so easily observed from the long stairs. Intrigued, she forgot all about herself and gave equal opportunity to both legs. Under what queer and unexpected situations I received my education!

Patty was so very thin that it was much more noticeable now that she was standing upright. Store-bought clothes hung loosely off her shoulders. While clothes are manufactured for chubbies, not enough children are so thin as to warrant the manufacture of "slimmies." So the sewing machine uncomplainingly served us further. I altered patterns and chose deceiving prints and styles. I was most grateful for the craft taught me by my conservative mother early in my high-school years. As Patty slowly gained weight she was able to wear tailored blouses and circular skirts. Since she slouched for a long time after she first learned to walk, the well-fitted clothes camouflaged the weak posture, inviting fewer curious glances. I wanted her trips into town to attract as little attention as possible. The braces naturally afforded us little privacy. On these trips I became introduced to pride's divine cousin, humility. I had to learn to ignore the eyes that followed the legs of my little girl.

The concrete walks of town were ideal for her walking practice. Patty's mind was busy with the exciting window displays. The curbs were an exercise in itself, off and on.

Added to the score of friends already won through Patty, we met another at the book shop. The woman studied her order books searching for simple coordination puzzles. When she heard that our Patty was walking, she couldn't contain her pleasure.

We returned to the Children's Hospital in Boston at regular intervals. New shoes were still being sent there to have raises put on them for correctional influences on Patty's walking. The standard heels were replaced with what is called the "Thomas" heel. Needed adjustments on the braces were handled at the same time.

We made regular follow-up visits to the Orthopedic Clinic where Dr. J could continue his observation of Patty's overall department. In the Fall, after Patty had been walking several months, I caught the doctor deep in thought as he watched Patty walk to and fro in that small room. After he had seen enough, Dr. J pointed to the braces she was wearing and said, "*They* did it. Remarkable improvement." I wanted to thank him for giving credit to something he had originally opposed.

One day I took Patty with me while I paid her

Daddy's insurance because in that particular building there was an elevator, something she had not yet fully adjusted to. Here, for the first time, I discovered her fear of doors! She pulled back as we approached the door of the office we were about to enter on the fourth floor. I explained that we were only here to pay Daddy's insurance. To her, any office in a professional building was a doctor's office. It was almost two years before she became convinced otherwise. And almost another year before she learned that doctors can be very nice people.

*S*he was five and one-half years old by the time she began to express real ownership. She was learning from Gail what fun it was to put the socks and underthings in their respective drawers. I was amused one morning to see her pick up her night cast (which had just been taken off her left leg after she arose) and put it in *her drawer*. It was hers, this cast, and she was scouting around the room to collect all her other miscellaneous possessions.

It was glorious to watch the development take place. I was ashamed for having come so close to losing my faith. We hardly dared close our eyes lest we miss something. Twice during the night we discovered good things were happening. The first time we were awakened about 3:00 A.M. to hear her humming merrily. The second occasion was to listen to her, alert as day, reeling off her entire vocabulary. So momentous was this, we dared not to comment aloud on it, Arthur and I. We reached out to each other in the darkness to clasp hands in prayerful thanks.

A new interest in words started only two weeks after she first walked alone.

***

*N*ew Hampshire boasts a total of 1,300 lakes, ponds, streams and I believe we passed 1,299 of them during the Sunday afternoons we drove about to make the most of our leisure hours. For these Sunday afternoons, Gail and I would pack picnic lunches and we would choose quiet little beaches at which we could swim. In her bathing suit Patty looked very thin, her legs especially so. Taking her to and from the water seldom failed to attract attention. This is the inescapable; families of the afflicted learn to live with it.

When autumn came, Patty had decided it was time for her to begin taking off her own jacket when she finished playing outside. She had learned by this time how to hold her own screen door open. Because it required such effort for her, I found it exceedingly difficult to watch her do it. She was very definite about wanting to remove her outer garments the same as Gail did. All this was extremely important to her.

I postponed the lacing of her shoe because it was the most intricate lesson of all. I decided it must wait. There were other more important things to accomplish.

"Patty has really blossomed," the psychologist voluntarily remarked, once the year had elapsed. The real self was emerging.

Back home, as one would expect with a group of children, they could be seen speeding past Patty while she joined them at play. When she fell my blood would chill. It would have broken Patty's heart to be denied the participation she was enjoying. I learned my own self-control. I watched our child learn to correct her balance, to brace her entire body to avoid falling as the other children raced by close to her shoulders. This child, so denied at birth, taught us what courage really is.

Despite all this progress, standing still demanded endless training. The three areas to discipline were her buttocks, her chest and her knees. My two hands needed an extra. If she had to stand still anywhere she would merely reel and fall within three seconds.

In early 1953, Patty began sending out whole simple sentences like: "I wan' Daune p'ay 'n eat here p'ease." "My boo' (boot) off p'ease," or "My boo' on p'ease." And for a while, "I wanna eat baby!"—her doll. Aunt Eleanor laughed and told her there had been no cannibals in the history of either side of the family and it would be better if she *fed* that baby! To which Patty responded, "Oh Dear!" her favorite exclamation.

On Easter Sunday, Aunt Claire arrived with two baby chicks for the children to raise. Patty grew especially interested in the chicks and they thrived all too well under the girls' care.

In three weeks time their wings took on such strength that they flew out of their box. Arthur and I watched the heartwarming sight of our handicapped child chasing them and bringing them back to their confines.

One Sunday afternoon we brought Patty close to where two ponies stood tied to a post reading "Pony Rides—10¢." Patty looked at her Daddy and said enthusiastically, "I wanna do that." Fully appreciating the opportunity, Arthur brought her beside the brown pony and handed the attendant a dime. As the attendant attempted to place our child on his pony, she stiffened and screamed. After a couple of months the opportunity repeated itself and Patty did permit the man to take her a short round with Arthur beside her. Although she was rigid for the whole distance, it was encouraging to see her helping herself overcome another fear.

Another enjoyable sight, about this time, was witnessing our other daughter prepare for her June Dance Recital. Gail never made any attempt to conceal her rapture as she practiced her arabesque, fouetté, and jeté.

She was more modest than Patty. Compliments would embarrass her.

At our next clinic appointment, Dr. J suggested that Patty go to school in September. I was astounded. She had not been walking a year and her speech was lacking; she fell often.

"Put her in; it's time," he said.

I began looking for a class beyond nursery grade without too large an enrollment, one where competition would not be too great. Having taken her past her fears and encouraged her self-respect we couldn't see throwing her in with a number so much greater than that which she played in at home. We could not risk her discouragement.

We listened to everyone's suggestion as to available

schools. We heard of a private day school run by the nuns. Gail was already attending a parochial school where classes numbered in the upper thirties. She was an "A" pupil.

The address given me was that of a not-too-familiar street, in the southside of the city. Opening the gate which surrounded the little cottage that looked more like a home than a school, I noticed a spacious play yard to the side. In answer to the bell I pushed, a Sister greeted me. I was invited into an office at the rear of the classroom. Sister apologized for the disarranged furniture, but it was spring vacation.

I sat in the seat offered me and started right in describing Patty's difficulties, her apparent incapabilities and her remaining few distrusts. I had brought her photograph.

"How large are your classes?" I asked.

"Well, in the past we have had very small classes, but with the closing down of so many kindergartens all over the city our classes have increased overwhelmingly." She was tactful, understanding, enthusiastic, but realistically frank. "We have enrolled twenty-three so far and it *is* early. Registration is not yet closed. We expect thirty-two." This was private kindergarten.

Sister continued, "We will be happy to have your little girl with us if you think we can do justice to all that has already been accomplished for her. Do think about it and let us know." As she handed me a paper she continued, "I am giving you an application with a return envelope for her enrollment if you and your husband decide such."

The Sister showed me the steps to reach the play yard, asking if Patty would be able to make those steps on her own at recess time. No, no, no. Sadly I reminded myself how often she fell in our own yard still where her playmates numbered four at the most. What would a rushing busy group of youngsters do to Patty's confidence?

No, this was not the school.

Searching the telephone directory, the only private schools we found featured day classes for little three-and-one-half-year-olds. It wasn't many days after this that our neighbor across the highway mentioned a relatively new school for special education. It was privately run. We lost no time arranging for an appointment.

Without Patty again, I visited the new school in its impressive location. It was in the northern part of the city, a converted colonial mansion. The schoolmistress invited me into one of the parlors which served as her office. I told her as much as I could about Patty and showed her the photo. The school's founding had been the answer to an ever lingering cry—children whose special needs cannot be handled by an already overburdened teacher—children having inferiority complexes, emotional set-backs, or problems resulting from illness or environment. The school enrolled a number of normal well-adjusted children as well. To my question as to how many in the school were handicapped, Miss W answered, "Every child is handicapped in one way or another in every school."

Registrations were strictly limited to keep classes small, to accommodate the special needs of each particular student. The tuition was high. I thought of our deplorably outmoded car which needed replacing. As a family, we had no luxuries.

I explained Patty's history of convulsions, adding that there hadn't been one for some time.

"She evidently is not subject to them often enough for our concern. But I am glad that you are being honest. It is quite a jolt when the teacher has not been prepared. Nor is it fair to the child who is put into the hands of strangers without advance warning."

She advised that we would have another two or three weeks to decide, before registration date. After discussion with Arthur, we decided that we would attempt it.

As fate would have it, I was not available to experience Patty's own visit to the school.

Instead, I underwent kidney surgery for stones my system would not rid itself of. All winter long, as I had grown pale and increasingly tired, I had paid very little attention to the sporadic, annoying kinks occurring to my right side. Other symptoms had come and gone until one evening in early May when Arthur insisted I join some friends in their invitation to an amateur play they were rehearsing that was scheduled for production in late May.

At the rehearsal hall I lacked any enthusiasm until halfway through the play when the lines came off so hilariously I couldn't contain myself. The kinks in my side became frequent and nagging until I couldn't ignore them. I didn't want to mention them to the girls as the play was coming to an end anyway. When the applause died down and I went to rise from my seat, I felt a strangeness about my leg on the same side as the kinks. When I tried descending the stairs to reach the car, I just could not make it alone. The puzzled girls helped me down the rest of the way, then into the car and into my own doorway.

Only the night light was on as I entered the house. Arthur had gone to bed early. I made up the sofa bed and slept there, in case I had any more of those crazy attacks in the night. Sleep never came that night. The mysterious pain in my leg grew worse and was relieved only when I decided to try elevating it. So, elevated it stayed until dawn.

Arthur was cross with me for not having awakened him and ordered me to call the doctor first thing after breakfast and get an afternoon appointment. It didn't require much convincing to have me follow his advice, for as soon as I tried to get off the sofa to start breakfast before getting Gail and Patty downstairs, I found I could not bear my right foot touching the floor.

I panicked. It had been exactly six years since the doctor had told me that there was a possibility the endometriosis might recur elsewhere.

"No, it's not endometriosis," my doctor informed me after a thorough physical, "but you should know better than to pass off lightly the presence of blood in the urine. Don't you know that you might have cancer?"

"CANCER!"

"Yes, cancer," he reiterated. He made no comment on my questions concerning that awful tenderness in my leg. Instead he picked up his telephone and called a local urologist. In the second man's office that same afternoon I learned that there were still traces of blood in the urine. I was admitted to the hospital the second Sunday in May. After four days of x-rays and other uncomfortable exploration, I was taken into surgery for removal of three stones from my kidney; miserable experience. When I awoke from anesthesia my body ached as though a thousand hands had wrung it out then left me there to die. After three weeks, I returned home. Mother had kept our girls.

Patty's Aunt Rose volunteered to bring Patty for registration. Grammy dressed Patty and curled her hair and Rose said she looked very sweet. At the entrance of the school, Patty began to chip at her fingernails from nervousness. She suggested to her Aunt, "You go in. I wait in car." Unable to contain herself,

Rose laughingly said, "Listen here, young lady, your grandmother didn't dress you all up pretty to have you sit in the car and let *me* do your business for you. You are coming with me!" After studying her Aunt, Patty had let herself be helped from the car. But, Rose said, she was timid and tense.

The schoolmistress made the visit very pleasant. Then to finish off the day, Rose took her into the local dime store where a high-pitched monotone was heard repeating "Hello! Hello! Hello!"

Patty, whose outgoing nature never permitted her to snub anyone, responded "Hello!" although she couldn't see who it was that greeted her.

The salesgirls laughed.

The voice belonged to the pollparrot in the cage overhead, reminding customers of the store's petshop department.

Chapter 10

Over the months of recuperating from my surgery, I was coming to realize that our two-story dwelling was too much of a hardship on my energy. We wouldn't be able to stay here much longer. The stairs, fourteen steps in all, were harder and harder to climb. There was only one clothes closet downstairs with no spot to build another. For the efficiency necessary to get Patty to and from school it would hardly be possible to remain at this address much longer. So Arthur and I began driving into town in the evenings searching for a first-floor apartment where we would be nearer whichever school we decided upon. Very soon we discovered the prohibitive rents attached to what we were seeking. We found only a four-room on the first-floor within our means. Discouraged, we decided to give it more thought before making any deposit to hold it. We debated whether or not we could adjust to such crowded quarters. Would it perhaps breed discontent in a family having enjoyed an airy country home? We voted to stick it out another little while.

By the end of summer we noticed a marked improvement in Patty's posture. So much so that I could shop successfully for ready-made clothes for her school wardrobe. As I shopped with Patty-Anne, salespeople edged over to us to comment on Patty's progress. Many of them had seen her on our educational sprees.

One day shortly after we had everything bought and ready for school, I was summoned from my kitchen by Cousin Lou. "Auntie Peg! Auntie Peg! Come watch Pat walk up the slope, all alone, without falling too!" Running ahead of me to Pat and Gail (another limb dropping off Patty's name as she was becoming one of the gang), he excitedly ordered, "O.K., Pat, here she is; show her, show her!"

Enthusiasm is every bit as communicable as childhood diseases. Pat, proud and joyous, began the difficult task requiring such absolute balance control. Gauging the sharp incline thoughtfully, she collected herself (part of her therapy lesson) and lifted her right foot just as I was pondering how only the family could appreciate the effort this venture required.

Lou and Gail stood on the graveled drive like two anxious trainers watching their young contender courageously climb that steep grade with a fierce determination in each step. She never once allowed herself to falter!

It was time for me to behave a little more placidly. A quiet gratitude was in order. We all knew each other so well now that we didn't need to speak our praise too demonstratively. Up to this point, it had been impossible to maintain our composure when Pat did something which to us seemed stupendous. Today, after a few brief words I returned to my kitchen and the children resumed their play.

During this same chapter in Pat's life when Gail

102

was through her bath she would shout, "Pat, would you please bring my loafers."

"Okay," we'd hear Pat answer, pleased at being put to someone's service.

"Now, my brush and comb," still gently courteous.

"Yes, Gail," respectfully.

As I remained inconspicuous at my ironing, I watched Pat tirelessly bring one thing after another to her grown and capable sister. It was a healthy reversal. Gail had served Pat uncomplainingly from time to time. Now she had decided by herself that it was time for her sister to become a little useful.

*L*abor Day weekend was over and Pat was thrilled to be in Gail's category; a school-girl! Her hours would be from one to three-thirty in the afternoon. Miss W's selection of the group including Pat was made with great care. It was a sub-primary readiness class in which actual learning is not hurried but encouraged individually. It was a class of six. As I brought Pat into the school and upstairs to her room, she left my side very nonchalantly to take the hand of Mrs. Z, a kind and motherly woman who had taught for many years. As Pat was led to the seat decided upon for her, I left the school with only a wink to the teacher, no "goodbye" to Pat. I have felt it a distinct advantage when wishing to avoid tears.

I walked slowly down the elm-shaded street. At this hour the autumn sun was just overhead and generously projecting its warmth on my shoulders. I felt such peace for all that was now ours. It was a day to review how difficult things had been and to appreciate the happy turn of events. I found myself recalling much about the past six years.

The session for Pat's particular class was a very short one. I then anxiously studied my watch to figure my time right, to be at the school when it let out. When I reached there, I was pleasantly surprised to notice my sister-in-law, Sylvia, and her Craig and Diane waiting to drive us home after this big day! Sylvia acknowledged my grateful signal. I entered the school to pick up our daughter. Immediately I noticed how ashen Pat's face had become since I had left her less than two and one-half hours ago. This new experience had made her tense. With a questioning glance to teacher, I was informed that Pat had done nicely. "One of our children cried half the session, but not *this* girl!"

At home, I noticed a little dried blood at the corner of Pat's mouth. The inside of her cheek had been relentlessly chewed until it bled. She had tried bravely to cope with this newest experience alone, without any member of her family by her side to help her. I asked the schoolmistress if Pat might be permitted to chew a piece of gum to help her over these early days. No. She would need to adapt.

Days after school first began, I was told by the teacher that when it was time to put books, crayons, and pegs away, Pat rushed so that she might help the others straighten out their chairs before leaving the classroom. I found this very heartwarming, since Pat was the only pupil in that group who bore a *physical* handicap.

Would that we could have watched this little girl in class! I was told of the small "band" made up of six classmates. Fife, drum, mirakas, accompanied the teacher's piano. Mrs. Z said Pat began shyly and self-consciously but within a few days became very adept at the toy instrument assigned her. Then action songs became part of their school day.

Pat's paper work showed very, very little, but we hadn't expected more.

*A*ttending school was establishing further independence and self-esteem in Pat. For me, however, the travelling by bus and making connections became exhausting. There was no alternative but that I learn to drive a car. Arthur shopped for and found a little inexpensive model. He tuned it up perfectly and devoted a small part of each evening checking it over to keep it in faultless condition. I never had to worry about the performance of that vehicle!

To cover the added expense I accepted a part-time secretarial job at the brace shop where we were having all Pat's work done. We had discontinued our trips to Boston Children's Hospital and Dr. J was doing the prescribing. Paul, owner of the shop, was another of Pat's loving benefactors.

The secretarial work helped keep my mind off Pat and gave extra purpose to my afternoon as well as easing the strain on an already stretched budget. The skilled workers at the shop were exceedingly patient with me while I struggled with the confusing language of orthopedics.

One Saturday morning when I brought some things up to leave in the storeroom, my eyes feasted upon what was going on in Gail's bedroom. Gail was lying flat on her bed reading a Polly Pigtails magazine, and Pat was *stretching Gail's heel cord*! Giving physiotherapy and saying, "Hurt, Gail. Hurt?" Gail was continuing the story she found so interesting, "Not too bad, Pat, you may continue," as she reclined there in king's daughter's style. They were typical sisters in several ways that we could now see.

In the middle of the following week I found the long-awaited answer to the slippering of Pat's feet. We were waiting for Gail's dancing lesson to be over. As I watched two little girls in tarlatans tying their slippers, drawing the strings up tight close around their tiny feet, I wondered why it had not dawned on me the very first time Gail had tried on hers? By now I was learning just how many simple things escape an overtaxed mind.

On Friday we purchased Pat's first practical pair of bedroom slippers. She became Gail's protégé. Nothing could convince her otherwise. Tenderly one evening shortly after that, Gail asked, "Pat, could you hold me while I do the backbend?"

How could Pat who weighed a mere thirty-four pounds support a sturdy girl like Gail? The request swelled Pat's ego. There she stood on the living-room rug, big as life, ready. Gail hadn't been kidding. She proceeded backward over Pat's outstretched arms. Then, just before Gail's palms reached the floor behind her, Pat's balance failed. They both toppled and burst into gay laughter.

After Pat failed in the tryout, I was inducted as Gail's partner for home ballet practice. I had to admit that after thirty, one's limbs do not have the same elasticity as a nine-year-old's. There was Arthur peering over the edge of his newspaper with an amused grin to catch my every awkward movement. Like the hydrangea bush, I should have been pruned each April.

*P*at's name for Mrs. Z in school was "Tee-as." Try as teacher might she remained "Tee-as" for the remainder of the year, telling me that through her many years of teaching she had been nicknamed often but that was by far the quaintest of them all. This was a special compliment because Pat avoided people's names whenever she could. Her Uncle Barty, however, wouldn't pursue any conversation with her until she made the effort to call him by name. Once impressed, Pat called him "Unka Bart" from then on.

It was not through lack of coaching that Pat refrained from some words or sounds. We helped her every day in attempts to correct or improve but she was not ready. It is only through the grace of God that her immediate relatives still speak a recognizable language. We almost gave up and adopted Pat's.

I noticed Pat exercising little courtesies on her own. As we closed our house each day and approached my car to leave for school I would open the door on her side and assist her into it. Once she settled in her seat I would go around the rear to the driver's seat. By the time I would reach there she would have my cushion in place. If it was raining she would start the windshield wiper as soon as I stepped on the gas.

She became at last a sightseer. The planes, the birds, the squirrels, the lakes we passed on our Sunday drives—she missed nothing! She listened carefully to the blue jays as they called to each other when our car crept stealthily across the picnic grove out back.

I became acutely aware of how close I was to crossing the limit of my strength where the housework and daily chauffering were concerned. In order to continue

we must have the accommodating arrangement of bedrooms, bath and closets on *one* floor.

Reminded of an endowment policy we had carried
since we were first married, we saw the means for
purchasing a home. As soon as we ate each evening
we piled into the car and drove about, looking for
homes for sale. It did not take us long to discover that
five-room, one-story homes sold for not less than $12,000
and we did not have the corresponding down pay-
ment.

Falling upon the idea of purchasing a piece of land,
we made a second discovery. We were concentrating on
quiet streets with little traffic to insure Pat's future
freedom. We learned that plots in our little community
were being tightly held because there were so few left
where city water was accessible. While our minds had
been focusing on our personal problems, considerable
progress had been made in our town heretofore not
on the New Hampshire maps.

With the altruism of a big brother, young Lou's father showed us a piece of his land situated on a very
quiet and winding lane where once he himself had entertained the thought of building. It was ours if we
could make use of it! We could now begin to build a
home. We had remained anchored long enough to see
our nervous baby through her tensions. She was not
easily shaken any more. With this assurance, Arthur
poured his concrete footing, then built his foundation
to set over the winter.

I had never seen Arthur so full of enthusiasm, so
buoyant. The prospects of becoming a homeowner—
finally! Even though he was now working harder than
ever there seemed no limit to his energy. He slept like
a kitten while I tossed and turned throughout the night
not at all sure that he would be able to swing the mort-
gage, property insurance, taxes, legal fees, not to mention two small loans not yet paid off!

108

His current income would reach $5,275.00. This was Arthur's sixth year with MSG & C Company, producers of aggregates and road materials for the construction industry. At their plant, Arthur was in charge of maintenance. I had given up my part-time job working for the brace shop to get figures for Arthur so that he was able to arrange all his own contracting. He had applied his own hand to almost every phase of the construction in his spare hours.

By mid-April the framing and partitions were complete. How marvelously curious Pat had been about the planning of this structure. While I went about my limited homemaking chores in the old house I found her scanning the building literature from the library and interrupting me to show a preference she had on windows and doors. Doors! This was the part of every structure which most intrigued her. Easy enough to understand; it was the only means of getting in and out of a place and since doors had held so much of the unknown for Pat, she *would* give deep thought to the design of such.

One day I found her measuring windows with her yardstick in our old house. Little mimic!

Excitement grew for all of us as the house was near completion. On Sunday Arthur would go to the earliest Mass, change into carpenter's garb and drive over to the new house. After the later Mass the girls and I filled one thermos with hot chocolate, another with coffee and drove into our rough terrain with Gail shouting a frisky, "Canteen. Canteen!"

Arthur would set up a makeshift table of plywood over sawhorses and we found our seats on surplus cartons of insulation. In the dwelling planned so carefully to meet our special needs, each new step was unfolding like a dream.

*I*t was now the first part of May and Pat's school had two days off while teachers attended a special conference on Exceptional Children, the new name given that group of children with unusual difficulties. The second morning, when our home chores were completed, we packed a light lunch and surprised Gail by being at her school when the noon bell rang. She joined us as we walked into the park across from the school and found an unoccupied bench. Pigeons promenaded before us in anticipation of any offering soon to fall. When we finished and dropped our last morsels to them, Gail took Pat walking in the park as I waited in the background, glad for a chance to sit leisurely. Gail proudly introduced her sister as she guided her through the playing throng. Pat kept looking for the Nuns.

When the noon bell called the children back into class and the park had become as deserted as the walks surrounding the school, Pat and I walked slowly to our car in silence. By this time of year each of us showed our exhaustion. We were forced to cut short the school year at the end of May because of it. Without warning Pat spoke, "Mom, *when* I go *their* school?" Although she had asked the same question long before, it was never asked quite this soulfully. I floundered. She was never demanding, always easy to answer when something just couldn't be. At this moment, I wished more than ever that my husband could be there to help me answer her.

"I don't know, Pat dear; we'll ask Daddy." Sympathy welled up within me. I couldn't tell her what it would be like to have to make her way with forty-five normal, active children.

When her Daddy returned home, she took matters into her own hands. "Daddy, when I go Sisser's 'kool?"

I waited for his answer with the same questioning look she wore. I had progressed no further than sympathizing. I had no answers. Two years in the special school had just not advanced her very noticeably, yet one should expect such things to take time.

Arthur looked at me, wondering what had brought on this question.

"Today we had lunch in the park across from the Sisters' school," I explained.

That one sentence was the entire story; he knew her love for the Nuns. But not sure whether or not to commit himself, he hedged, "When do you *want* to go to the Sisters' school?"

"Now!" she replied.

"Well, I guess you know what you want. We'll see what can be done about that, Pat," Arthur said, disarranging her hair with an affectionate stroke of his hand. Gail was standing close by and there was no mistaking her pleasure.

It was decided at that very moment without discussing any pros and cons. Arthur felt it was worth taking a chance.

I wasted no time securing an appointment at the private day-school operated by Sisters, several streets away from Gail's school—the school I had visited two years earlier.

Mother stayed with Pat while I kept the appointment for late afternoon. I was invited into a small, plainly furnished room. Waiting twenty minutes, I grew apprehensive. Suppose we were wrong. She did so need special education.

The door opened quietly and a sober searching-eyed

nun looked over to where I was seated. I rose and introduced myself.

"How do you do, Mrs. StCyr. I'm Sister Mary Carmel," she informed me sedately.

I carried with me a folder containing Pat's school work. I reached into my handbag for the photograph of Pat for Sister to see and while she held it in her hand occasionally glancing at it, I explained the several factors which impeded Pat's performance; her undeveloped motor skills and her perceptual difficulties. We had yet to learn the specific approaches necessary. Her mental development had been aided significantly by the stimulating experience of school-life.

"You realize, Mrs. StCyr, that compared to Patty's recent specialized schooling, our program will present a contrast?"

"Yes, Sister, we do, and we are a little frightened by the fact. But we are wondering if any reasoning of ours will seem logical or important to Pat herself. We are even more afraid of what we might stifle by refusing her this wish. It might be time to gamble. For the first time in her life!"

Sister weighed the situation thoughtfully.

"Very well, Mrs. StCyr. Since you and your husband have prepared yourselves, why don't we arrange a time for you to bring Patty in for us to meet her?" Pat would be the only party in this arrangement free of doubt.

The second Sunday in May was the day designated by Sister Mary Carmel for me to bring Pat in. Mother's Day! I had made some slight improvement on my appearance in order to save the children and Arthur from the temptation of denying their affiliations with me.

With Pat beside me, I slowly climbed the steps which led to the glistening white face of the convent entrance graciously designed to offset the somber red brick of the rest of the building. We waited expectantly after

112

hearing the ring echoing on the inside of the convent door. A tall pleasant Sister answered. We announced that Sister Mary Carmel was expecting us.

As we waited in the small reception room, Pat and I chatted aimlessly. When Sister Mary Carmel greeted us, she was holding a blue plaque of the Blessed Mother. She knelt to Patty's forty-three inches and embraced her with unrestrained tenderness, handing her the chosen gift. Pat was ecstatic. My warm tears rebelled at my efforts to conceal them as I watched. Sister rose and for the first time I was privileged to feast on that beautiful smile of hers. Laughing, she remarked as she looked at my hair, "You look so different!" I hadn't thought Sisters noticed the proud.

Pat, not wishing to waste precious time, said "Show me my room now, p'lease," despite our having explained that her enrollment here was only a possibility! Since Pat's words were very often muffled, her statement was not clear to Sister Mary Carmel. At my clarification, Sister laughed again. "Well, I can see you never dally, Patty!" she said as she walked hand-in-hand with Pat. Sister seemed strangely delighted walking with her, almost as if she had been asking guidance of Him and had just now received it.

After spending generous unhurried effort in exploring carefully Pat's knowledge as they sat leisurely beside one another, Sister sent for her superior to sanction such an enrollment. If Sister Superior felt any reluctance, she kept it well hidden. She outwardly approved as she assured me that our girl would make out all right.

Before we left, Sister Mary Carmel succeeded at something I had tried and failed at so continuously; "Sis-ter, Sis-ter, Siss-ter, Siss-terr", she said until Pat responded without fault. My optimism returned, convinced of the influence this particular Sister would have over her pupil, our daughter. With the three of us testing Pat on the stairway, it was concluded that the hazard would not be as great as they had imagined.

At the door, Sister Mary Carmel said cheerily to Pat, "We will see you in September, won't we Patty?"

Exuberantly and enunciated carefully, the response went "Yesss, Siss-terr!"

Chapter 11

Gail's recital time was set for the first Friday of June. Gail would be doing the Highland fling with her partner, Helena Hughes. They would be wearing red plaid, taffeta, pleated skirts, royal-blue, long-sleeved, jackets with wide, interfaced cuffs and pointed, peplum flaps ornamented with gold, tinselled half-inch ribbon. The cuffs and peplum flaps required a total of twenty-two arrowhead points which I had never attempted before.

I was visiting the dance school to check with Miss Howard, the dancing teacher, to see if the costume was going along as she wished. Across the room Gail was conscientiously going over the pert Scottish routine with Helena. Pat was with me, absorbed wistfully in the dancing practice. She wanted so much to join them. One particular high-school aide, dressed in leotard, studied Pat. She walked over to me and asked if I would permit her to give Pat dance instruction in the adjoining room. I explained carefully (so that Pat could not be hurt) that with her faulty balance Pat would not for a long time be able to dance.

"Well no matter," said Cynthia Dunbar, the teenager, "I'd really enjoy going through simple instruction with her in private. And I know *she'd* be happy," she added, smiling at Pat. "I've watched her eyes as Gail dances. Pat wants to dance so badly. I'd be willing to stay in town after school any afternoon you find it convenient to bring Pat. I've already asked Miss Howard."

I was touched beyond words. This young girl, pretty and popular, wanted to give of herself, so genuinely. As I switched my eyes to Pat, I saw her with her foot already up on the chair, unbuckling the calf-band of her braces. I had lost the argument.

The weekend before the recital I had to bring Gail to our local auditorium for the last rehearsal. Pat and I waited in the seats out front as Gail went backstage to join Helena. While we were being entertained with the numbers by the tinier tots, we knew that the older ones were nervously rehearsing behind the curtain. In the middle of the small-fry, rag-doll number, Gail skipped out front to Pat and me to tell us that Cynthia wanted to see us backstage. Curiously we walked up the steps to reach Cynthia who was all smiles over whatever it was she was holding behind her back. "I have a surprise for you, Patty!" she said.

"Let's see," exclaimed Pat.

Cynthia pulled out an exquisitely theatrical, red-satin costume with row upon row of net ruffles that sparkled with gold dust. Three of us stood breathless, realizing it was for Pat!

"Cynthia, where did you . . ." But without allowing me to finish my question, she was stealing Pat back into a quiet distant corner to see if it fit.

116

"My Mom made it," she called out, "and Miss Howard furnished the sparkly net to finish it off real elegant!"

Once in it, Pat was a shining young star. For all the brilliance, who could be aware of a handicap? We were beginning to learn that Pat was more realistic about her limitations than we would have ever guessed. She would be content with just trying. The thought that such a fluffy ballerina dress hanging in the closet belonged to her would amply serve as her fulfilled dream.

*** ***

*O*n the fourteenth of July we moved into our new modern home boasting six-foot closets with sliding doors, a bath with shower and archways leading from the hall to the kitchen and living room. There wasn't one single threshhold to impede Pat's travel from room to room. Our tomcat, however, failed to share our ecstasy. He remained merely overnight, devoured the breakfast Gail graciously served him, and once let out, found his way through the wooded knoll back to the familiar, two-story grey house. Disdainfully, he loitered under the porch there until, with no other alternative, the new tenants adopted him.

We were now utterly exhausted. The days had been pitilessly hot. That first night with what seemed like our last ounce of strength, Arthur and I made our way out to sit on the narrow step of our front entrance. We sat there appreciating the silhouetted beauty of motionless aged pine enhanced by July's last-quarter moon and expressed our sentiments to each other. When we returned inside, the children were giddy in their chatter. We wondered if ever anyone had been as glad over a new home.

Arthur heard a commotion the next morning at quarter of five. Upon investigation, he discovered Pat heading toward her closet, choosing a dress, laying it out on her bed and busily walking back and forth. She seemed so thrilled, he said, that he took her into the kitchen with him where she sat beholding every feature of the new kitchen exclaiming how pretty it all was, despite the walls, yet to be painted, and the unvarnished woodwork. Before she became too wide awake, Arthur escorted her to her bed with instructions to go back to sleep.

Over on the avenue adjacent to ours a neighbor just happened to have a kitten recently weaned and housebroken, which we fell heir to. He was prettily marked, mostly black, which inspired the name, "Sabu." We were pleased that he harbored no prejudice concerning modern ranch houses.

For the balance of that summer Pat experienced the joy of playing beyond the scope of her mother's intervention. While I only allowed short periods of this, in fairness to Gail, Pat was perfectly reconciled. She played very contentedly with her doll and carriage once Gail left her to join the company of children her own age.

It was such a noticeable change as we readied for school. Pat's previous schooling had been afternoons and while mornings now would give us less time for dressing, the conveniences of the new house more than compensated.

It was very reassuring to know that her mornings would no longer be idle and the best part of her day would be applied toward learning.

118

She was no longer restless in the night. Her improved appetite was a thing we could rejoice over and colds were no longer sapping her energy.

She walked into her schoolroom that first morning a very happy girl. Sister had her desk chosen the previous day when she invited us in to familiarize Pat with the new surroundings. I departed almost immediately leaving a phone number where Sister Mary Carmel might reach me if she had any problems whatsoever.

At 11:15 when I returned to wait outside the classroom, I could hear the recital of noon prayer, an added feature of Pat's school life. When Sister opened the door to allow the children to file out, she told me Pat had made out very nicely throughout the morning. "However, while the children stood for the prayers, Pat just about lost balance. Will she be able to stand through three prayers?"

I suggested she stand for one, perhaps.

Though I did not feel Pat could physically stand the morning and afternoon session, Sister suggested we try it. After three days of it, Sister informed me that Pat looked spent, consequently making little effort at anything.

Once the first grade was sufficiently organized, Sister Mary Carmel began leaving her door slightly ajar. Through this narrow space I peeked without the children spotting me. I tried often to be early reaching the school to observe Pat's application during class. The attention she paid was remarkable. While she was given pages to color with a few others on this type of assignment, another group did oral work at the front of the room. Pat was not the least distracted during all this. Too absorbed in her own assignment!

One morning Sister asked me if Pat knew her colors.

119

I said "yes" because I knew she did. But it was a strange thing; Sister told me that when she specified that Pat color an object red, invariably it would be done in yellow or some other color. I couldn't explain it because at home if I suggested she wear blue socks, she always chose the right color from her drawer, or a green dress, she picked it without fail from her closet. (It was some years before we realized that if a sudden manual performance is expected or a direct question be asked, Pat to this very day can't often be her most accurate.) Nevertheless, following Sister's discussion with me, we began reviewing regularly with crayons until Pat became more consistently accurate with her colors.

Her coloring improved slowly due to her poor coordination and she seldom finished one object before she hopped to another. At home we were stern while encouraging her to finish whatever she began.

She repeated making her numbers as shown in her sub-primary grades but we still saw no evidence that she knew the value of any given number.

Several days had passed before Sister mentioned anything more concerning the prayers. Pat had complied with Sister's wish that she remain seated until the group arrived at the shorter prayers. Then one day at the beginning of prayer, Sister saw Pat get up with a look of defiant independence, struggle until she affected good balance and when Sister paused, Pat declared, "I *stand!*" defying argument. I might have been embarrassed over such arrogance except for Sister Mary Carmel's sporty appreciation over any new sign of development in Pat.

When the majority of the class began reading, each pupil was asked to stand with his First Reader in hand and read word after word. Sister didn't call on Pat since Pat was unable to read. Occasionally Sister reported to me sadly that Pat raised her hand and said, "Sister, I 'read that!" When Sister encouraged, Pat would stand, study the page, and then admit, "I oney foo' you, Sister."

Sister felt deeply moved and repeatedly expressed the wish, "If only I knew how to help her; I feel she has half a thought and then loses it before she can express it."

I reassured Sister that everything else had required a great deal of time in raising Pat and we could not expect reading to come easily. I tried to convince Sister Mary Carmel how pleased Arthur and I were with Pat's growing nonchalance despite the competition in class. That she was still self-confident, we could not be more thankful.

Certainly Sister's overwhelming effort in Pat's behalf was unparalleled. From the unique things she suggested I try at home I knew that when she retired to her quarters each evening it was a long time before she sought rest. She made up picture cards from pages taken from one of the First Readers, and penciled the spelling of the object beneath for us to use at home along with the extra set of flash-cards she made for us. She tried ceaselessly to unlock the combination to our daughter's confined store of knowledge, blending patience with devoted understanding. We knew how very much she wanted to help Pat.

On her own set of flash-cards for Pat in school Sister lettered the words in bold black ink on a yellow background. When time arrived for her to assign her class written work she would call Pat up to her desk to begin teaching each word taken from the first part of the reader. Pat would guess without really trying at first. As this practice was repeated she began to be more serious at it. She appeared to understand, Sister reported, although her responses did not back up the appearances.

The week following, when Sister passed the arithmetic problem papers around the class, and was just ready to give instructions on same, she heard, "Sister, Sister!" Turning around, she spotted Pat's hand raised.

"Yes Pat?" wondering what was wrong.

"You no give me one ' *those* papers."

Uncertain how to handle it, Sister's mind was racing. "Oh Pat! We wouldn't forget you for anything, now would we?"

As Pat thanked her for leaving one for her, she answered, "I hope *not,* Sister."

While Pat solved none of the arithmetic problems she wanted it clearly understood that she should be given a chance.

One morning the class was asked to tell about their pets. A boy rose and told how his pup chewed any slipper he chanced to find. A girl told about her fluffy little kitten. A boy described his parakeets.

Each child couldn't wait to tell his own pet story.

Pat's habit in class was that of listening. Her interest this day reached such a peak that she could no longer sit in her seat passively. She envied all the appreciation each storyteller received. When the last one was finished and it appeared to Sister that the story-telling period was over, Pat raised her hand. "Do you have a story, Pat?" asked Sister.

"Yes, Sister, 'bout my pup," with new seriousness.

"Is yours a good puppy, Pat?" she asked invitingly.

"No." Her classmates sat curiously up in their seats wondering how powerful would be their slower friend's narration.

Pat obviously noticed the excitement she was stirring for she continued, "aannddd", dragging it out for effect (which too was new), "he ' in my bedroom, and my mother ' *mad.*"

The class enjoyed it. While Sister expected that

to be the end of the story, Pat cashed in on this mute applause so new for her in class. Drawing her eyebrows together in a scowl, " 'n, know what, Sister?"

"No, Pat, what?" Sister herself was eager for the suspenseful installment.

"He s'eeps wi' my father!" The children rocked with laughter. The little fabricator! Little had we ever expected the day would come when she would resort to falsehoods to capture a listener!

That was the beginning. It wasn't long before she took a definite stand in our living room one afternoon when I asked her to please step into the hall while I vacuumed.

"No, I work. Wait p'ease," she said matter-of-factly, forming three's and six's on her paper.

I repeated gently, "I need to vacuum, Pat; I'd like it if you would go into your room just long enough for me to do a quick job here." I confidently unwound the cord of the vacuum before plugging it into the outlet, convinced she would be leaving as asked. I looked up. She was making no attempt whatsoever to uproot herself!

"Patty-Anne, did you hear me?" I said more sternly this time.

"Mmmh hmmh," without looking up, "but can't move now; not done."

This impudence coming from Pat?

"Would you like me to take you by the ears?" I challenged.

Chuckling as only she can chuckle, she began packing her pencils into their box and straightened out her papers without hurry.

She walked out into the hall past me and leaned against the wall still enjoying her little joke. "Mommy, I just foo' you!"

While Arthur shaved that evening, I related the incident of Pat's arrogance to him. "Now, what are you going to do about that?" I said, feeling him out.

Wiping his razor and grinning, he did not surprise me. "Not a thing. Not a thing. We've been waiting too long for her to become like the others."

Chapter **12**

*I*t was now late October. Russet and gold leaves lay thick on our lawn. A capricious autumn wind sends an impetuous deluge of top-leaves scurrying past the avenue as I returned to the house after taking Pat to school. The trees facing our front windows resemble whisk brooms. The night before we had had a torrential downpour. The glorious blaze of color was no longer with us.

Now it is time for Goblins and Ghosts. Trick or Treat. The air is crisp and I shiver for the little tykes who will be out parading in their imaginative garb this night. I have filled the big wooden bowl on the hearth with cheery MacIntosh apples, wrapped caramels and other chewies. Black and orange motifs hang on our stark-white unpainted walls.

I wondered about the half-mask laying nearby that we had purchased for Pat exactly like the one her sister would be wearing to complete her last year's gypsy costume. Would Pat overcome her fear of the mask to wear it even briefly? We doubted that she would. Gail continued to insist that Pat share the excitement of Halloween. So I dug out what colorful fabric and trim I could from my sewing remnants and threw together gaudy attire for a diminutive gypsy. This year proved little different from the others. Arthur and I wondered again why insist that Patty wear a mask if she dreaded it so?

I guess it was to please Gail since she never stopped deriving gratification from Pat's inclusion in her games. Gail was only a fifth-grader. By the time she was to finish elementary school she would be convinced of the things over which Pat might never have control. It should not be strange that Gail couldn't accept it for so long when even teachers before and since could not easily refrain from urging Pat into such functions because "all children like this kind of events."

In November from casement windows in the northeast corner of our kitchen we stop our breakfast to feast our eyes on the wild pheasants in our marshes nearby. First came the proud handsome male endowed with all the beauty from his black-barred brown tail sweeping the ground behind him to the ringed, irridescent green plumage gracing the head which peers, eagle-like, north and south for any likely threat to his obedient ladies. They cautiously await his signal from their lookout between the season's tall, dried grasses adjoining our lot, a natural camouflage for the duller flecked female pheasants who blend advantageously in the dormant fields. Within seconds in response to their master's assuring call they appear one behind the other, serenely strutting toward him behind the thickly grown fir boughs which crowd each other grandly hedging our avenue. We were certain that this was not within our neighbor's design when he originally planted his long row of spruce and fir.

But that doesn't stop game from popularly seeking their shelter there away from rambunctious hunters.

There were so many things to be glad for on this new avenue. I remember one morning Arthur's shaking me awake to "come quickly and see the deer!"

I rolled over apathetically. From all the doings of the new house, I hadn't the least intention of dragging my weary bones out of bed for a mere wild thing. At a more reasonable hour, of course, I would have with lightning speed, loving nature as I do.

Schoolchildren were selling Christmas cards competitively in the weeks that followed. It started us wondering where we would set up our tree. For the ten years in the old house, it had without exception shone from the front window. Never any question.

"It's got to be a big, big one, Dad, for over there," Gail insisted as she pointed to the side window in the living room. Arthur said "Yes, at least a ten footer!"

The room measured seven feet, six inches.

It would be lovely there with its full lower boughs resting on the window bench concealing the first wrapped, secret gifts we would not so frugally purchase for our girls. A clock-radio for their Daddy, maybe. He'd been wanting one.

With all the gay felts and corduroys currently on the market, I could sew the cousins gifts if I stopped all the daydreaming and hurried more.

As soon as Gail and Pat were off to school next day I dressed in ski togs and lined boots. Hunting season opened December 1 and I was becoming more afraid each year to venture into our deep woods after that date for the princess-pine which grew so generously there. The tiny lush-green pickings could be strung in a rope around our wrought-iron lamppost that the electrician had just wired up. With what was left, I'd fill the holly-bowl Eleanor had brought us from her recent trip to California. Indeed "sugarplums danced in our heads" introducing our new house to the Season of Christmas.

We had not yet lit our new fireplace. When we did on December 5, we forgot to remove my wicker planter of philodendron from the mantle; it had taken me three years to grow! From all the smoke we amateurs produced it withered and died within the hour.

On the twentieth, now within the octave of Christmas, we opened the cartons of tree decorations. The antique silver balls from Uncle Fred's attic weighed so heavily in our palms. We had plans to have a design handpainted on them with Gail's and Pat's names sprawled across in frosted lettering. For now we'd hang them plain on the sturdiest part of the tree.

Next we pulled out the chorus of ballerinas in gold and blue which we had traced and carefully cut several Christmases back to embrace our yuletide tree. We'd virtually forgotten all about the chimes and miniature organ we had once used for a centerpiece. Up they went, replacing the dead philodendron. They fit perfectly and gleamed when the lights played upon them.

The tree that Arthur bought was not quite ten feet but it was taller than any we had ever had before. Our decorations were all used up before we got fully around the tree. So we loaded the deprived branches with boxes of silver icicles, stood the white gowned angel at the very top of the tree, corrected her posture fussily, and straightened out her tinselled wings, cramped from the year's inactivity. We then set up the Manger Scene. Mary and Joseph knelt beside their newborn Son while shepherds revered closeby. Sheep stirred. A star shone brightly. Bethlehem!

128

The hour played its own hymn.

Flames in the hearth shot upward from logs Arthur had added to the paper. Our family sat dreamily back enjoying the spirit swelling our hearts, inevitable peace bursting anew, recalling the age-old story of Christ's birth.

New Year's Day came and went, then school resumed for Gail and Pat. The roads were treacherously icy but we got through thanks to our faithful Chevvie.

Then came a day in March.

I arrived outside the classroom where Sister Mary Carmel was waiting for me. "Would you have an extra moment so that I might file all the children out and talk with you about something, Mrs. StCyr?"

"Of course, Sister, I'm not in any hurry." But I was annoyed at how my heart raced. I became nervously apprehensive. Everything was going so well. Was there something now to spoil it? Please God, NO!

"Come in," she said after she finished with the other children. I had hardly spoken to Pat. "We have something to show you," she added.

"Tell your mother what this word is, Pat."

Without glancing up at me once, "Loo-ook," she obeyed slowly.

"And this word?"

"Bay-bee," she answered thoughtfully.

"And this one?"

"Fa-ther."

Without further asking but merely flashing the cards before her, Sister allowed her pupil to take over the rest.

"Oh!"

"Mother."

"See."

"Tim."

"Work."

Sister Mary Carmel looked to me and questioned, "What do you make of *that*, Mother?"

I couldn't speak.

*C*ards spelling out new words were scotch-taped all over our walls. Pat was now reading "upstairs" and "downsevers" for "downstairs." This struck us all very funny; it could never be explained why she said one so perfectly right, and the other so ridiculously wrong.

At home we were getting ready for Gail's twelfth birthday. She had already invited a few of the girls from school and the rest were her neighborhood girlfriends.

As always we used the St. Patrick Day theme since her birthday is only two days before. The Kelly-green foil hats in miniature were pasted on to individual place-cards and we would serve early supper. Open, hot beef sandwiches with gravy, then the cake.

What would the skies give her, this birthday girl grown suddenly chubby with adolescence? A heavy, nine inches, of snow.

While Pat amused herself inside, I grabbed a shovel and cleared a path to the front door, noticing only later that it is these small emergencies which can heighten the fun of a party. How easily we forget this fact.

Gail's guests arrived with her immediately after school. Arthur was home by the time I was lighting the candles with the enthusiastic assistance of Cathy

130

Houle who rated high on Gail's list of close friends. Cathy was blossoming into a captivating beauty with snapping black eyes and blue-black hair.

Arthur greeted each girl in the inimitable spirit which he reserved for his "hello" to nice ladies of all ages. The girls continued their celebrating in the living room while Arthur, Pat and I ate in the kitchen. Spring would soon be here if we just shut our eyes to that snow. And with it this year, Pat would be making her First Holy Communion.

At our new parish, St. Catherine of Sienna, we enjoyed a far closer relationship with the clergy than we had known before. Father John Foley never failed to remind Arthur and me to come into the rectory for a talk at any time or hour. Often he threw out little words of praise or comment on Pat's improvement. He would tease Gail every chance he had about becoming a nun.

On May 27, following her ninth birthday, Patty-Anne would join the other slightly younger normal girls and boys in their well-rehearsed procession down the aisle of our parish church.

I remained through the two initial rehearsals to answer any problems of Pat's over which the nuns might become concerned. I was myself not without worry. How would Patty-Anne do, her scissor-gait what it was, braces and all? The feet toed in decidedly. Everyone wondered how she kept from tripping herself. The knees knocked one another as she walked.

In other situations she was almost always safe with one of her family or a teacher guiding her by the hand. At home and school she could touch a desk or wall when she guessed she might fall. Between cleansings, our walls carry the mute testimony.

But the Sisters had also thought of these things;

two "Guardian Angels" were put in charge of our daughter. Although they were Patty's exact height they were three years her junior! How would they manage?

As I'd learned to do, I excused myself from the church and went to a nearby supermarket. My apprehensions were thus drowned in the process of my marketing.

Father Foley was certain it was going to go off without mishap. He laughed off whatever doubts the nuns and I entertained.

We all knew Pat could not be included in the long procession around the block outside the church preceding Mass. Consequently, they arranged for me to sit in the very last pew with Patty until the last two children would halt at our reserved pew. It would be at this moment that we could expect the two "angels" to take Pat's hands and walk her down to the pew where she would stay until the Offertory of the Mass.

The nuns suggested that Pat's father and sister sit in the sacristy within close view of the altar in the event that Patty became ill.

Pat listened with great interest to catechism instruction and was growing impatient for her very important day. She was not alone in her enthusiasm.

Very early in the planning, her godfather, Roger, had asked if he and Stella might be given charge of her dress and veil. He was looking forward to designing both personally, in the Boston bridal shop he commuted to daily, in the capacity of production manager, where he accepted the position following his training at designer school. Uncle Paul insisted on furnishing the white shoes to match the lighter weight aluminum braces with snug calf-bands of new white leather from Aunt Eleanor.

It had been about this very same time that Mother

had mentioned hoping to be allowed to buy the dress.

Roger and Stella repeated their request two more times, but for fear of hurting Patty's grandmother, we couldn't quite relent. Understandingly, Roger gave up the designs dancing around in his imaginative brain. (They would have to be saved for his own daughters, of which he now boasted two.)

He asked that we show him the dress, as soon as we chose it so that he might start on the veil.

That first exquisite item was found at Carter's Children's Shop, next to the stationery store on Hanover Street. Mrs. Carter, the proprietor, waited on us. She already was so familiar with Pat, from all the hard-to-get items she had located for us.

"This is a special girl," said Mrs. Carter, "so we have to find a special dress." She went into the back room and returned with a one-of-a-kind dress of frothy lace. It fit Pat perfectly. Mother and I looked on delightedly.

"I want to give it to you at cost," Mrs. Carter said. "I would never enjoy any profit I made in this instance. With this dress I wish all God's love and blessings for your girl. She has earned them."

Roger designed a petite Juliet cap from which he would drape soft veiling for his godchild.

With all the preparations for Patty's First Holy Communion complete, I couldn't help but reflect seriously on the Gospel of St. John read on the Third Sunday after Easter: "Amen, amen I say to you, that you shall weep and lament, but the world shall rejoice. You therefore have sorrow now; but I will see you again, and your heart shall rejoice, and your joy no one shall take from you. . ." The grave hours, days, months of our child's existence when answers had come always so slowly, the years interminably long—and now she was to receive her First Holy Communion. No one could take our joy from us.

The morning came. I found it overwhelming that not one of us, Arthur, Gail, Pat or myself, commented on the rain falling outside our windows! In our hearts no rain *could* fall. The day was *all*.

In church the last blond oak pew to our left was bedecked with white satin streamers put there by the nuns—for us! Arthur raised the padded kneeler to admit his braced daughter into her seat with me following. He gave her right wrist an affectionate squeeze. Then with his equally precious Gail he proceeded in the direction of their designated places in the sacristy near the altar.

Patty-Anne fondled the glazed decades of her new rosary beads. She couldn't say a complete prayer; not even a complete sentence from a prayer, but her memory carried the entire message of the *Our Father* and the *Hail Mary* even though, aloud, it was only the key words to these prayers she spoke. Always in their proper sequence, however!

Her lace cap level with my shoulders, her face lighted by a glow befitting the occasion, Patty earnestly tried to control her curiosity, turning often to see if the procession she was to join was anywhere in sight.

A hymn I knew so well touched me deeply as I recalled its sacred lines while the organist rehearsed it softly:

"O Lord, I am not worthy. . . . "

I prayed for composure. Before I had time to get nervous Mother and Eleanor appeared and sat close by in an adjacent pew. Down the aisle, we caught a glimpse of my brother John with Sylvia, his wife. Tapping us on the shoulder from behind was Arthur's white-haired Aunt Mandia, his favorite aunt always. Shortly afterward Roger was accompanying Stella with her miniature color camera, down the outside aisle.

A handclap was heard from outside. It had come

from the two nuns directing the now visible long line of children, bringing them to an abrupt halt while the final instructions were whispered. The waiting parishoners stood up to witness the inspiring sight of trained boys and girls filing into the church. Devotional music appropriately received them. The rain, reduced to a mere mist, silhouetted the continuous trail of white illusion veil. The boys with meticulously combed hair, their mischief poignantly absent, were sober and soldier-like, their two hands pressed symbolically heavenward.

As the end of the line was fast approaching Patty and I saw the two little girls dressed as angels eagerly glance toward us. My heart skipped a beat as I turned to lead her out of the pew and deliver her to this pair of winsomely inexperienced children, sweetly dressed in powder-blue floor length dimity. Their haloes glistened twice as brightly as their starched, frosted wings.

Not a second was lost as each of these petite girls grasped Patty's hands and ushered her with all the caution of adults to her given place alongside the others at the front of the church.

My cheeks were moist. Guardian angels, seen or unseen, were seldom on any day far away in this life for which God in His love and wisdom had made our second child so different. Patty-Anne would never have to walk alone, any more than she was walking alone this Trinity Sunday.

Voices hushed. Mass began. In white vestment festively trimmed with a wide band of glimmering gold, Father Foley bowed low and made the Sign of the Cross. He then ascended the white marble steps to the altar and on it spread the immaculate linen on which the holy chalice was to rest. From our missals we prayed privately: "We beseech Thee, O Lord, by the merits of Thy saints whose relics lie here and of all the saints; deign in Thy mercy to pardon me all my sins. . . . "

Then the Introit: "Blessed be the Holy Trinity and undivided Unity, we will give glory to Him because He has shown His mercy on us. O Lord, our Lord; how wonderful is Thy name in all the earth!"

The Epistle included the words " . . . Oh, the depth of the riches of the wisdom and of the knowledge of God! How incomprehensible are His judgments and how unsearchable His ways! . . . "

The two last lines penetrated my heart. "There is beauty, God"—the tangible improvements in our Pat, those we could see and touch; those were what mattered, those were what brought a closeness in our family we could not otherwise have known. And the joys! Oh, the joys!

The Gospel was finished and the officiating priest was saying the Offertory Prayer. Father Foley prayed in a low voice, blessed the bread and wine with a Sign of the Cross five times, consecrated the Host, then the wine, and elevated the chalice.

It was time for our children to approach the altar rail. The children received the Host in rows of half a dozen abreast. Three girls on the left, the same number of boys on the right, in the order in which they had left their pews. When the final row was close to being all served, the "Guardian Angels" escorted Patty-Anne toward Father Foley. They waited obediently at the foot of the altar.

On the top step of the altar, Father Foley waited. The angels had been instructed over and over again to procede no further than they were at this moment. But Father Foley had other ideas! He beckoned the three girls forward. The steps could pose a hazard for our daughter. Panic seized me as I witnessed Patty-Anne take the initial steps toward Father Foley. How

136

were Gail and her father reacting to this tense moment? Literally an eternity.

Patty made it. Father Foley placed the Host, affectionately, on Patty-Anne's tongue. " . . . *Suffer ye little ones who come unto me. . . .* " Patty-Anne backed slowly down the steps. At the rear of the church I swallowed the lump in my throat.

At the end of Mass when all the normal boys and girls had filed past where I stood, I caught the blissful face of our Pat. Her hands were clasped and she walked between the guardian angels completely independent of them. A new scapular hung from her shoulders and she was wearing an air of triumph. Arthur and Gail, looking extremely serene, reached our pew where Pat sat beside me. Before saying much to us, they rushed toward the departing "angels" to thank them for a job so well done!

The next day, back at school, the nuns described the anxieties they too had suffered, unprepared for Father Foley's ignoring what had been so carefully rehearsed.

"Just like a man," one of the Sisters interjected, with more than slight exasperation. "Just *like* a man!"

*T*he close of the school year came without much fanfare. I was, as always, looking forward to the rest that summer brought.

In September, we returned to The Mount where Sister Mary Carmel continued to give Patty-Anne as much individual attention as she was able. At home we were offering more words on cards.

By January we realized that it would not be long

before the time spent in Pat's behalf might be questioned by some of the other parents. This was not a school for the afflicted. Yet, Arthur and I knew that every bit as much attention was given our child as she had received at the privately owned school where she had spent her first two years.

I could see that it was beginning to sadden Sister Mary Carmel. More time was needed and her present class was larger this year. If Sister's health allowed, I fully suspected that she would be teaching only exceptional children. On days when I commented on her pallor, she would dismiss it casually until a few days' absence would convince me that she suffered some chronic ailment. Because our association had over the two years reached beyond a routine parent-teacher thing, I was able to learn of the internal malfunction which was confining her to her bed on some school days.

During conversation one day she told me about the Joseph P. Kennedy Memorial Hospital in Brighton, Massachusetts where Patty-Anne's worsening orthopedic problem might be re-evaluated. Arthur and I, of course, had every confidence in Dr. Hagerty's word, that surgery *was* necessary—something in the ankle region of both feet called a "triple arthrodesis"— but that he strongly objected to its being prematurely done. That might make the repeat of such surgery mandatory at an older age. "I will not have these kids go through it *twice!*" he said.

Since her feet were becoming more and more crossed it was requiring increased attention on all our parts to keep Pat from tripping herself and ending in a fall for one or both of us. On January 23, I sat down and wrote the letter to the Kennedy Foundation. The Order of Franciscan Missionaries of Mary operate this rehabilitation hospital. In only six days we received a

138

reply signed by Reverend Mother Mary Joannice, Administrator. It was a form letter, describing their facilities, their evaluation fees, and requesting a letter of referral from a physician as well as records from hospitals and clinics attended.

We felt little or no enthusiasm—we expected no miracles. The mimeographed summary of their facilities stressed the fact that while an educational program was offered during the patient's stay there (provided by the Boston Public School Program), Kennedy Memorial was not, in actuality, a *school*. A child is accepted for admission primarily on the basis of his medical and therapeutic needs. Upon completion of these needs his discharge is immediately effected.

I went through the exhausting routine of obtaining records and requested another appointment with Dr. Edward Hagerty, in order for him to give the most up-to-date appraisal of Patty-Anne's condition. The New Hampshire Crippled Children's Services provided a written case history of her therapeutic achievements at our local rehabilitation day-center. Then a letter from the Manchester Sisters of Mercy.

By April 23, I had been there and back with Patty-Anne.

It was an impressive center and the examinations were thorough, with gentle, friendly nuns and uniformed specialists.

I had never seen so many crippled children in one place. It appalled and weakened me. There were so many types of brain-injured children. I was not fully aware of how it was affecting me until the woman who was giving me a guided tour of the various departments touched me tactfully on the shoulder and solemnly asked, "Would you like to see our next department, Mrs. StCyr?" Only then did I realize the stunned state I was in for several minutes. Spina-Bifidas with heads hanging over the sides of their wheel-chair; a few with overgrown heads, with only a short life ahead; some legs so crossed that one wondered how they ever got separated. As we walked down the corridor, I realized my guide must have grown very accustomed to her visitors' reactions to wards like this. While I reflected, a twelve or thirteen-year-old girl, seriously afflicted and heavily braced crawled along the walls to reach her destination.

I was pale and spent at the end of the tour. I welcomed the near-hour's wait in the office of the department chief, who was to give us our answer.

The doctor spoke with me alone. What he told me was not news. The first thing they would undertake for Pat would be surgery, followed by long braces for the legs. Academically, she was very limited, they concluded. We had already imagined so. They would consider her admission as soon as I discussed the matter with my husband.

All the way from Brighton to Boston I remembered those others. And counted our blessings!

Arthur and I didn't take long to make our decision. We would wait until Dr. Hagerty felt it was *time* to operate.

Chapter **13**

*A*nother year was gone. We were beginning to feel the pinch of being new homeowners. Not to mention all the other things! Before finishing payments on one small loan in February, we found ourselves negotiating another one to keep our heads above water. With overtime Arthur's earnings had reached $6,223.01 before taxes. And I, with the optimism of every would-be writer, decided to submit some of my light verse which up to now I had written for pleasure. There was quite a bit of it tucked away in a desk drawer, a stationery box, a building manual, the girls' baby books. Spare dollars were not going to come from that effort. Suffice it to say that my verse is so light, it just *flies* off an editor's desk.

I was spared further disillusionment when in midsummer an old friend of ours who ran his own agency in real estate and insurance, phoned the house to ask if I could substitute for his regular girl while she vacationed for two weeks. Mother agreed to take

Pat, and Gail was reliable enough to leave home or in the immediate neighborhood under her Aunt's loving eye.

It was only after considerable deliberation that we had decided not to enroll Pat *anywhere* for school this year. She was ten years old now, and a third year in Sister Mary Carmel's first grade somehow seemed not quite fair to teacher or pupil.

I devoted an hour or two each day running through flash-cards and simple arithmetic. With us alone in the house without distraction it seemed the ideal learning situation. She thrived on single attention and learned quicker with it. Was this not even better than special schooling, where several handicappeds are taught in the same room, by one teacher?

I could not be that teacher, for long, although Dr. Hagerty asked why not?—Because I was finished. My duties involved more than just being Pat's teacher. Gail was growing into a young woman. Soon she would be entering high school. Her life would be more social. Arthur's working hours were long. The emotional strain and work involved with our new home and grounds left not enough time or stamina to consistently plan a program of tutoring for Pat. Tranquility is a must and I would not pursue the job on days when I did not possess it.

I was beginning to feel the terrible injustice to families with children of limited intelligence. At the New Hampshire Child Guidance Clinic, we were told Pat's I.Q. measured 72. The norm is 100. The 72 classified her as an "educable" child. The merely "trainables" were those registering under the 50 mark. In the city of Manchester with a population of 90,000 there was only *one* class for the slow or retarded child provided by the public school system. In our town—population 3,600—there were none. In Manchester teachers were available for the homebound. In our town there wasn't one.

I joined the newly-formed group of Parents of the Mentally Retarded. In the years as member of Parents of the Crippled Child we dwelt on the social and physical limitations. But now with Pat's age and school history we had to learn all there was to know regarding her opportunities as an intellectually retarded child.

This was the year to separate the handicaps. It was made positively clear that certain avenues open to the crippled child possessing an average I. Q. were closed to our daughter with her multiple handicap.

By November 25 I had a letter off to Mr. Murray H. Watson, Superintendent of Public Schools. He lived in Candia, a town east of our own. My letter gave a clear picture of Patty-Anne's needs and limitations.

In just a few days, his reply reached us:

Dear Parents:

Before I can grant your request for a home-teacher, it will be necessary to obtain all the information available concerning Patricia Anne's case and take the matter up with your local School Board.

I have already taken steps in the latter direction, and you may be assured that I shall do all I can to help the girl. You will hear from me just as soon as I am able to tell you anything more.

Sincerely,
Murray H. Watson

Shortly after a kindly woman-principal appeared at our door, ready to start work with our elated Patty-Anne. Her name was Mrs. Josie Bean. It was 3:30 P.M. The end of her school day in the village six miles north!

143

Could we expect the lessons earlier in the day soon?

"I'm afraid not, Mrs. StCyr. You see, I have to be available for all the issues that are presented to a principal. But I assure you that I will give it all I have. Other teachers were approached on it. They would be paid by the hour, of course, plus their mileage, but none of them volunteered. The travelling alone would take them home so very late."

Merely another fact of Pat's life—and the life of the many thousands born each year in states where no mandatory law for their special kind of education is provided! In every population, however, there are the Josie Beans. Like Sister Mary Carmel, she was zealous and made progress with her pupil from the start. Pat adored her and on the two days each week that she knew Mrs. Bean was coming she would be excited from breakfast time on. I saw Mrs. Bean glow with pride when Pat learned something new. She was deeply moved that this child could not be provided with more regular tutoring.

"It is sad, terribly sad. We see in our encounters, some parents who aren't *enough* concerned over children failing their grades. And here you and your husband have made these sacrifices; yet a town offers only this very lacking bit of help now that your resources are running out."

Inevitably, this too had to come to an end. Our town had no full-time home tutor. Mrs. Bean needed to devote whatever time she had to her salaried role as principal. "But I would certainly approach the School Board, if I were you and Mr. StCyr. You are not transient people."

Transient? Hardly. Arthur's parents had paid property taxes in the town for thirty-two years. My forebearers had owned land and property here since long before 1893 when Grandfather William O'Donnell

144

granted land to the School District of Hooksett on which they built their very first one-room public schoolhouse.

"You must be heard, Mrs. StCyr! I will give it my wholehearted support when the matter is brought up at whatever meeting it might be proposed. Patty-Anne deserves more hours' attention than I can give her." Then, after a pause, "How high is the tuition at the private school she first attended?"

"I understand that half-days has gone up to $300 annually plus $10 for books."

"Well, put your request before the Board, and good luck."

We would do that for the following school year.

As a member of the new Manchester Association of Retarded Children, I was attending lectures, helping with the initial fund drive, talking on allotted radio time to awaken the listening audience to the existing needs of the known retarded of our communities, selling tickets to benefit shows, viewing documentary films, and driving to conferences on mental retardation to represent our parent-group and bring back reports. (I was one of the few mothers with no pre-schoolers, with a car to reach the distances, and helpful Mother lending her enthusiasm in the matter of rehabilitation.)

It was now 1958.

We were not successful in influencing Gail to take the college course, despite the fact that we had an endowment policy on her since birth to provide for higher education. She continued to insist that she wanted to become a secretary. She wanted to begin her training right now. It was hard for us to accept since she was so very studious. The nuns kept insisting that she was college material. Gail was such a studious child, her homework coming before anything else. During her freshman year when school dances began and local social activities for teenagers were initiated, she announced to us, "Except for holiday affairs, I'm not going to be able to go out on week nights. Otherwise I can't do justice to my studies."

We were overwhelmed! "Well, you know best, Gail." Who were we to argue with thinking such as this? Then she began taking more and more time to help me about the house. Her friends came often to the house, styling each other's hair, having snacks, or planning an occasional party. Football began to interest her. Sundays meant earlier dinners a bit more rushed to have her ready for friends who dropped by to pick her up.

We received the answer from the Superintendent of Schools regarding Patty-Anne's enrollment into special private school; the Board had voted to accept the responsibility for her tuition. The closing of the letter by Mr. Watson was warm and sincere.

The school was now in another location, another stately mansion. The lawn was spacious but the room for Patty-Anne's class was very small and crowded. Arthur and I were taken aback when we saw the very narrow aisles and desks lined up against the wall. The teacher's desk had little room around it for our daughter's free movement. It was not the least bit like the spacious, sunny room she had originally had when the school had a smaller enrollment. More and more normal children were filling the new school. We immediately learned that no pupil could enter from the street level; everyone first went down the narrow stairway to the basement to hang his clothes and his lunchbox there, then came up to class by still *another* stairway.

For Patty it was apparent this would be increasingly difficult; her feet were crossing more and more.

Side by side we would have to descend and climb those designated stairways each morning and noon.

In September it was hard to envision what walking in that long driveway would be like come January and February. I couldn't help but wonder how the single blind boy was expected to make it on those bad days. He was chauffeured by some enterprising housewife who collected fares from each confined parent and who drove off without a backward glance when her vehicle was free of the young passengers.

With each year we were discovering the hard, unpalatable facts: *Survival of the Fittest.*

Perhaps it wouldn't be too long before Dr. Hagerty would decide it was time to operate on Patty-Anne. In the meantime, we tripped together a few times when it was treacherous underfoot, or when Patty-Anne was tired. But encouraging words I had memorized from last spring's State Conference on the Mentally Retarded (the first one ever held in our state) echoed in my ears to sustain me. I had listened passionately to the provoked experts crying out for more legislation and community spirit on behalf of its retardates. They were the forgotten ones, confined to a life of nothingness unless the parents could or would send them to whatever private school existed in or near their localities.

What about the *others?* The one class provided by the Public School System of Manchester, New Hampshire's leading city, took care of merely twelve of these. God only knows how many hundred there were at home. No complete census of them had yet been taken.

At the Conference in Concord I took down notes for our new Parent Association. Just after ten o'clock, Dr. Herman Yannett led the speaking.

He was an Associate Clinical Professor of Pediatrics at Yale Medical School and Medical Director of the Southbury Training School in Connecticut. He was a strong proponent of integrating the retarded child into the community, terming it "true deprivation to institutionalize these children," to separate mother from child as many doctors recommend soon after birth.

"There should be special classes in the center of the community, not only on the elementary level but on the high school level as well. Even the *normal* child, without a school program, without a recreation program, will become a child with problems such as we see with the mentally retarded who are not offered an education; seventy-five percent of the mentally retarded are educable!" he exhorted, raising his voice heatedly.

"In Hawaii," he added, "public nurses fly to remote sections *to help parents* with a mentally handicapped child."

The most *expensive* way to handle persons so afflicted, he said, is in institutions. The more adequate and least expensive way is in the home. Where institutions handle thousands it is nothing less than a monstrosity. Day to day, in the community, stimulating programs can and should be set up.

"It is important for parents and friends to join groups, to push legislation," he said. "Legislation does not move by itself!"

Returning to the issue of retardates being raised in their own homes, he explained:

"When parents themselves take these exceptional ones into their hearts, so too will their other offspring. When the family as a unit accepts this 'different one,' the neighbors will follow suit. When the neighborhood gives him his rightful place in its circle, the entire community will do likewise."

148

I caught myself nodding unabashedly in the affirmative; it had been our experience exactly without a single exception. But I honestly had to wonder about those afflicted children who had such serious behavorial patterns that the neighbors' children were often too frustrated by these unfortunate traits to *continue* including a retardate not able to control his tantrums and offenses. Here again, the harsh realities. It would be even so with a neighbor's normal child whose temperament raised havoc among his playmates. Neither would he be graciously accepted.

We had been particularly blessed in Patty's outgoing disposition. Her love for all begot love in return for her.

One of the speakers at the Conference was Father Richard O. Boner. As well as being pastor of a busy Concord parish and Camping Director for the Diocese of Manchester, he was most popularly known for initiating a week-long camplife for crippled and retarded children in New Hampshire's scenic Belknap County.

It had germinated from a brainstorm of two non-Catholic doctors. Under Father Boner's influence, volunteers from colleges of law, theology, medicine, and practical education, nuns, nurses, and high-school seniors, swarmed to the Camp Fatima to serve as free counselors to the many boys and girls, campers of all faiths.

This conference left much food for thought on all that was left to do to improve the lot of our retarded. Its encouragement and guidance would provide the push that many of us needed.

At home our minds were shortly taken off ourselves, at the news that a sister for Cousin Louie was on the way. For thirteen years he waited, not to mention the equal longing of his patient parents. They had been resigned to having an only child for several years now. When she arrived in late February, she was perfection itself. She was everybody's baby, this Kathleen. A tree in her honor was planted by "Uncle" Arthur the day of Kathleen's christening while Gail and young Lou were joyfully standing as the teen-age godparents a short distance away.

With passing months, Kathleen showed unusual intelligence. Her brother was reading to her long before the usual age. Any contact at all that we had with the child left Arthur dreamy-eyed and overcome with envy. Thank *goodness* for the fifteen cousins who followed Patty-Anne, the cherubs who inspired:

In Our Garden of Cousins

A garden that grows and grows
Always a new bud shooting up
Falling heir to attention from those
Who by now are growing like ivy
Hardy as autumn straws
Our need it is to pluck the weeds
Which create their private wars
Some are the fair and gracious
A few a wee bit frail
We pray that when they adolesc
Our pride in them prevail
Whether in a crowded city
Or "suburbia" you fare
You must have such a garden
They grow . . . just *anywhere*.

I had been dismissing her "Do I have to go tomorrow?" But it was repeated frequently as we'd walk slowly out the paved driveway from school to our car.

I would reply, "Why, of course. Everyone has to go

tomorrow, unless they are sick. You sick?" I would challenge.

"Nope," That would be that.

It happened altogether too often. So one afternoon, I ventured, "Why do you keep asking that, Pat?"

"I dunno." She wouldn't elaborate. I imagined that she might be growing tired of such repetitious work or feeling it wasn't worth it for the little new she learned. The challenge no longer existed.

Chapter *14*

Summer came and went. Eleanor had just purchased a six-room camp at Lake Winnisquam on the waterfront. This was where most of our weekends were spent. The uncles rebuilt the sagging pier while the many cousins swam, basked on rubber floats, or slowly rode across the lake in the aluminum boat. When any of us felt in the mood to, we picked up a paintbrush and brightened a wall or two. How grandmother loved these Sundays! She constantly cheated on her strict diet.

In September, Pat and I would begin a lazy year with the lack of a class within the radius of our own town. It was obvious that except for the right residential school, if one could be found, her school life was over.

In the city, the hard work of the parent group, with the steady encouragement of many interested friends, was bearing fruit at last. A classroom was set up in the chapel annex at Grenier Air Force Base under the guidance of Capt. Irving Tulin who had a retarded child. Through him, Colonel T. K. Hampton, commanding officer, contributed the use of the annex. It would serve 12 retarded children screened from a number of 44 during the summer.

There were indications that city funds might soon be made available to shoulder the financial burden. Mayor Josaphat Benoit, at the formal opening, was heard to say that the taxpayers should be able to provide *some* measure of assistance, that it shouldn't hurt anyone too much, since the city spends several million to educate children in the public schools. The school was named "William J. Moore School" after the president of the United Commerical Travelers, a fraternal organization which had adopted the cause of the mentally retarded.

Classes would be held five days a week with half-day sessions accommodating two different groups. The category chosen from the 44 children screened were the "trainables" since these were the ones totally neglected by the public school system.

At home, this would begin the first year I was not to be a slave to a clock or calendar.

Pat was now twelve years old. Her orthopedic problem was now serious enough for us not to grieve over the academic.

Gail began going to formals and dating occasionally. At St. Joseph High, she was a member of the choral group and took part in the musicales with great enthusiasm. For dances which the school held she would consistently volunteer for one committee or another and contribute something toward its success. Patty-Anne gloried in Gail's variety of activities. It was not at all rare for her sister to sit patiently at her bedside after a fun evening to fill Pat in on the interesting details.

Pat's own day consisted of television shows and

her phone call to her grandmother. Some days she and I rode up to Stella's or Louise Merrill's for a chatty afternoon. Pat didn't seem to miss school.

Now was an opportune time to have her teeth taken care of completely. The dentist who had been cleaning them regularly over recent years and painting the pinhole cavities with silver-nitrate until such time as Patty-Anne's nerves could stand the necessary drilling, found himself overwrought after actually filling one.

Patty could not open and close her mouth immediately upon request. Her tension in a dentist chair resulted in maximum spasticity. There was the risk of the filling drying before the job was complete. Understanding the dentist's difficulty as well as our daughter's sincere attempt at cooperation, I too became nervous.

While the nurse made out my receipt and I helped Patty-Anne on with her coat, she tactfully suggested that I take Patty-Anne to Boston Children's Hospital where they had special methods and facilities. The mere mention of Boston recalled too many of the hard days and sent shivers through me. It seemed we had come so far since those times. I thanked her, but I would certainly not resume my trips to Boston. In earlier years it had been the only thing to do. In this instance the answer might be found with a younger dentist. It was worth exploring.

In Dr. L we found our answer. He was young, and so low-voiced that one had to strain to hear him. He had soothing music playing throughout the office. His nurse was only a few years older than Gail and her voice wasn't any louder than the dentist's. My visit beforehand, alone, had warned Dr. L what his trouble would be. He exchanged casual words with Pat to let her see what his office was like and what he himself was like. Then he gave her the date on which he hoped to see her, not once looking over at me. This swelled Pat's ego.

Pat looked very smug as she took her seat in the car headed for home. She and Dentist L hit it off beautifully. He placed a hard rubber block in the back of her mouth to hold the jaws apart while he worked. Onto the lower front teeth he hung the tube serving as a saliva ejector. He talked slowly about anything to his spastic patient while his fingers worked methodically with minute particles of moist filling. I could hear Pat answering him with a muffled "aha" each time it required a response. Each time he moved away from her to mix filling or lean over for the drill or polisher, she would anxiously look back toward the door for me. I remained there out of the conversation. Doctor was doing magnificently.

The following visit he tackled an extraction by merely freezing the necessary area. She did not fight as he injected the needle into her gum! She trusted him implicitly. Lightly, I accused him of practicing hypnosis. He smiled.

Patty was tiny and looked much younger than she actually was. As most people do, he regarded her as a very little girl even though her age was in his card-file. "She gave me no trouble at all."

For the visits after that, I stayed in the reception room, to enjoy a magazine. Patty-Anne was so proud that she could walk the foyer approaching the dentist chair without assistance. We remained with him for the dental work. It didn't take long after that to have her teeth in A-1 shape. She consumed far fewer desserts, candy and soda than did her normal sister whose more independent life exposed her to much of it—soda pop and record hops being inseparable!

*D*uring the next April, at Mass on the second Sunday after Easter, Fr. Dow at St. Catherine's mentioned Camps Fatima and Bernadette, both sponsored by the Manchester diocese. Camp Fatima was an all-boy camp. Camp Bernadette, all-girl. He described what each busy day included, in the way of land and water activities, competition and counselling.

He concluded, "If you know of some child whose family might be interested in learning more about the matter, we shall welcome their inquiry. The camp is for children of *any* faith or race. Exceptional Children's Week, for *both* sexes, is held at Camp Fatima only."

Following Mass, Fr. Dow gave me the address of the camp's assistant director, a Paterson, New Jersey address. We received a prompt reply to our letter and with it routine forms to fill out for familiarizing them with our daughter in all areas of her handicap; the extent of self-care, eating and sleeping pattern, social adjustments and fears. Part of the questionnaire was to be completed by the applicant's physician. If the application was accepted, we could plan on the week beginning June 19 and ending the 25.

On May 16, we kept our appointment with Dr. Edward Hagerty. That visit brought us back to something temporarily overlooked; Patty's surgery.

After examining Patty and walking her, Doctor reached a decision. "It is time to operate." I was startled! Fortunately, Pat had first been escorted to the waiting room before he returned to discuss it. I mentioned her application to the camp. All right. Should she be accepted, he would operate as soon afterward as practical. If not, he would schedule surgery sooner.

While it was exciting news, it held doubts. Success could not be guaranteed one hundred percent. (Arthrodesis meant surgical fixation of a joint by fusion of the joint surfaces. Triple arthrodesis meant that three joints in the ankle would require fusing.) "But I have done it on several Cerebral Palsied, with gratifying success," he said. "I will give you their names. If you and your husband feel skeptical of it, you don't have to go through with it."

Planning for camp presented a temporary escape.

By return mail we received a list of items she would need to bring: bed linen, a pillow, four blankets, one heavy sweater, warm pajamas, raincoat, and rubbers.

On Monday, June 19, Gail and a girlfriend accompanied Pat and me to Gilmanton for her first experience at Camp Fatima. Her clothes and bedding were marked and stacked in the trunk of the car. A small bottle of phenobarbitol was in my handbag to leave there with the nurses. Pat had not needed any for a long time. But it would be her very first time spending a week away from home with a busy schedule and much excitement.

We went over the scenic route, awed by the varying greens and blues of the valleys with their contrasting hills and distant mountains. Across the breathtaking horizon, rich white clouds rolled lazily. We almost passed the small sign reading "Camp Fatima." I turned into the narrow dirt road darkened by rows of statuesque pine standing like sentinels to guard the campground entrance.

We stopped for lunch on the way up. It was now 12:45. Registration was from 1:00 to 3:00 P.M.

158

It was overwhelming to witness the faces of the waiting staff; a rare contagion of happiness exuded from every direction! Young counselors were renewing friendships of summers past. This was the program's seventh year. 109 children were expected today.

Seminarians, nuns, student nurses, all roamed the grounds, impatient to meet their new charges. Cars yet to be unpacked, once cabin numbers were assigned to the excited perspiring car passengers for whom this trip was expecially made. Handshakes taking place wherever the spectator paused. Perhaps one day Camp Fatima's goal—an entire summer season for the handicapped ones—would be reached. Never would a Christian spirit be better illustrated.

We introduced ourselves to enthusiastic Mr. Barker, Chief Counselor, who had been responsible for accepting Pat's application. "We're so happy to have your Pat with us, Mrs. StCyr," he said. We could see half a dozen gentle riding horses within the fenced circle just ahead of us.

The camp boasted thirty-three cabins. As we left the registration desk, we were handed a lined index card with the counselor's name and the cabin number. Which would be Pat's cabin? Number 33! We got back into the car and followed the directions to the modest white building where our new camper would sleep and rise for the next seven days. As we stopped the car three sociable young women walked curiously over to us. The tallest of the three said, "I'm Mary Ann Sposini," as she briefly glimpsed the leg braces worn by Pat. "Who is your counselor?"

"Mary Ann Sposini," I said referring to the index card.

"How do you do," she smiled, "I am she," and to Pat, "I will enjoy this week with you Pat," who returned with "Me too!"

It would take less than another five minutes to discover why the counselor seemed to recognize her camper the minute she saw her. Miss Sposini was from Massachusetts where she attended college preparing to teach the mentally retarded.

Counselor and camper were now hand in hand. With all the introductions over, Gail and her friend helped me with the luggage and blankets. Two of the counselors whose campers had not yet arrived helped open the screen door for us. Mary Ann had already walked Pat over to her empty cot where she could sit while we talked. There were cots on both sides of the large room and a bathroom close to the entrance of the camp. Every alternate cot was made up with narrow wool blankets and percale-covered pillows. These were the counselor's cots. A round-the-clock watch was kept on each child.

One girl kept her back to us and never stirred when we came in. She was seated on one of the furthest cots. A few of the girls struck up friendly conversation with Gail and others were interested in Pat. Soon the dark-haired, silent girl rose from her cot and turned to face us. Our godchild, Vivian Villemure, in tartan plaid shorts and cool sleeveless blouse stood there smiling at us. She and her mother had purposely kept the secret from us. She would be graduating from Sacred Heart Nursing School later in the summer and knowing Pat would be arriving with the scores of handicapped ones, Vivian asked to be given the same building where her young cousin would be.

"Of all the wise ones!" I said airily to her. Pat was elated over the discovery of her cousin's presence.

As we were leaving Mary Ann was putting Pat's raincoat and summer topper on hangers, and Pat, half-eager and half-confident, shouted a command to

160

us, "Send me a card," in the monotone which gave her away.

"We promise," we replied and left abruptly, knowing she would, once relaxed, find all these fine young volunteers very interesting. She would hardly miss us.

Before leaving the country road, we took longer glimpses at the herds of volunteers finding a variety of ways to help the gravely afflicted who were arriving in such number. The athletic-looking young people assisting were maneuvering wheelchairs so skillfully it seemed as though they had done it all their lives. There was little hesitation or awkwardness regarding the condition of the arrivals for whom this camp week was so inspiringly designed.

With peace and lingering astonishment still flooding our minds, we reached the main road. To return home so early, on this divinely beautiful day seemed unanimously a shame, so we went sightseeing through Gilmanton, past grazing fields and old homes well-kept. All *country*, hitherto serene and sabbath like.

Yep! We felt sure that Pat was going to enjoy one whale of a week.

All of that it WAS. There were boat rides, sitting atop a horse, attempts at craftwork which for Pat were quite limited, entertainment in various forms over at the recreation hall, and motoring around the campgrounds with Miss Sposini at the wheel of her car.

When Arthur, Grammy and I went to get Pat the following Sunday there was no mistaking the fact that she had become homesick, just as her more normal contemporaries would following a week away from home. She literally climbed on us to embrace us hungrily. Her tired, drawn eyes were conspicuously moist. Were not our own?

Arthur was introduced to Miss Sposini and in turn

161

introduced his mother-in-law who held Patty-Anne enclosed in her gentle embrace.

Mary Ann was full of compliments on Pat's cooperation and behavior. "But she sure became lonesome a few times. That letter from home meant so much to her. She showed it all around," and looking fondly on Pat, "Didn't you, Pat?"

Pat nodded and wandered slowly with her grandmother to point out the nearby chapel where she had proudly received holy communion with the others each morning before breakfast. Campsite #33 offered a long view of the entire compound.

While Mary Ann was telling us how much it had meant to her to learn about a child both physically and mentally handicapped, a car full of male theology students drove up and glanced over to Pat's direction to say "Goodbye." Recognizing them Pat smiled at them and tugged her grandmother toward their idling car.

"We'll be saying a prayer for the success of your foot operations, Pat," we heard one of them say as he shook Pat's hand. Arthur and I looked helplessly at each other; we had purposely not discussed surgery with her prior to her week at camp. Miss Sposini's eyes were sad and apologetic. Wincing, the young theologian realized what he had just done. With the facility of a seasoned Shakespearean actor he brushed a sweaty brow with his left hand and mustered a smile for a second shake to our daughter's hand exclaiming, "Hope your summer is full of a lot of nice things, Pat."

"Thanks," she responded mechanically, robbed of the pleasure such an encounter might otherwise have carried. She had heard his every word, from the very beginning. She stood frozen and defenseless.

The collegiate driver shifted the car and drove off quickly. Grammy led Pat to a seat in the Rambler. Mary

162

Ann kept repeating her regrets, explaining that she had mentioned Patty's forthcoming surgery one evening during relief period at the recreation hall when fellow volunteers were discussing the many differences in their cerbral-palsied campers. "I'm sure it is my fault," she said. "I never thought to add that your daughter had not yet been told how soon surgery was being planned."

Arthur and I felt almost worse for Mary Ann than for Pat.

"After all this time, Mary Ann, we can hardly expect no slips. Pat's life holds many kinds of unpleasant shocks and surprises. We would be telling her in just a matter of days, anyhow. The main purpose was to give her this week-of-all-weeks spared of such news." We meant it sincerely. *How* we would tell her had just been taken out of our hands. We would now need to carry through, however bluntly, once her short simple questions were thrown at us, possibly as soon as we got into the car today or at least before we reached home.

"We'd like your mailing address, Mary Ann. It's so hard to tell you how very much we thank you for the help and friendliness you have shown our Pat. She'll be talking about you all summer long. Some of this you might enjoy hearing."

While she was bending down to scribble her address for us we left our gift-wrapped token on Pat's undressed cot. As suspected, the trip home was long and painful. The dreaded subject was handled with callous honesty. No other choice had been left to us. She shed no tears.

"When?" she jabbed solemnly.

"In two weeks, Pat," Arthur swiftly answered when I hesitated. It would be exactly ten days. But Pat's vague conception of dates made it easier for us. It was kinder to phrase it in weeks.

Grammy remained mute. She knew her voice would crack if she tried to talk.

163

In my handbag, I already had Dr. Hagerty's letter dated June 22, directed to the hospital:

Patient's name: Patricia StCyr
Diagnosis: Cerebral Spastic
Marked bilateral equino 'varus deformity
To be admitted to hospital July 6
For: Triple Arthrodesis on Saturday (8th)

Five deadly serious lines. Arthur and I realized its full impact. Dr. Hagerty had explained it all carefully. He would cut below the outside ankle. When surgery was completed, he would put the leg in a cast from the toe up to the groin. The second operation would follow the first by about a week.

"How long will she be in a cast, Doctor?"

"Three to four *months*."

"Months," he repeated without any change of expression. I think he hated its necessity as much as we did.

"However," he added more kindly, "at the end of about eight or ten weeks, we shorten the cast to knee length."

It was a small consolation, but any would do for the time being.

"Do we take her home before her second operation, or only following the second operation?"

"Following."

"After the second operation, will she be able to walk in those casts?" She would not be able to master crutches. The reciprocal motion demanded for a tricycle years before was one of the most difficult feats of Pat's life.

"One week after her first leg is done, the nurses will stand her up, put a canvas shoe over the cast and her brace on the free leg to see what can be accomplished."

164

"Will we be taking her home in short casts?"

"No. After the second operation, it will be from bed to chair. And a bedpan."

"Any more questions?" Dr. Hagerty asked compassionately.

"Enough for now."

Chapter 15

*T*he only thing of which we were very sure was the surgeon. He had saved many a life and innumerable limbs deemed hopeless by lesser men. He was tops in his field of bone surgery. When he gave an order, he accepted no excuse for its not being carried out to the letter.

We remember the time he was twisting Pat's foot this way and that to confirm how bad it was getting over the last two years. She had been sitting on the edge of his examining table, her legs dangling.

While his head was bowed seriously studying the feet, she lifted his horizontally-striped tie out of the snug-fitting vest and said, "You have a nice tie, Doctor."

He never lifted his eyes. "Glad you like it, Pat." As he indeed might have with adults, Dr. Hagerty was never known to overlook a child's statement, whatever trivia it contained.

How hard it had been for me not to smile on such occasions.

For our July 4th weekend, Eleanor invited Lou, Rose, John and Sylvia with their children and us to her Winnisquam Camp.

John brought along sparklers for the small children to light and enjoy from the pier once dark would settle in. A far cry from the "Fourths" we had known as children, with bags of rockets, firecrackers, and all the rest, with our dad enjoying them even more than we did. We engaged in a wild discussion about the more modern hazards encountered by today's children almost daily and wondered why the new law prohibiting fireworks for one holiday only had to be so permanently stringent as to rob this new generation completely of all the fun we had known on nights before the *Fourth*.

We didn't break or change any laws that weekend, but it was far from dull. I take that back. Grandmother broke her diet rules. As always when she got up to the camp she was overcome by sights of tempting picnic-table spreads. We had to admit to each other that during the days that automatically followed she suffered not at all. It seemed the outdoor meals improved her state of mind, for whatever the risk they might have been to her high blood pressure. Her one great happiness was being surrounded by all her grandchildren on the holidays, not hosting the group any longer, but enjoying them none the less. Her days of setting large tables and filling pieshells to please all tastes were over.

Following church on Sunday, Bart motored down from miles up the lake, where he was just clearing his wooded campsite before building. He came down with his five-year-old, Jim, and by turns took the family out in his faster, more powerful boat.

With all the shouting and laughter, we didn't have to think about hospital and operating rooms, reserved for four days from now.

168

But since all good things must end, we drove home in a virtual caravan late Monday evening, on Interstate Route #93.

We reached home safely, but tired.

As scheduled we brought Pat to Sacred Heart Hospital on Thursday and she was admitted in satisfactory spirit. Once our Blue Cross identification number was taken down on the records by the Admissions nun, alongside address, telephone number and name of parish, we were escorted by the records clerk via the elevator up to 6th Floor Pediatrics.

A cheerful red-haired Irish nurse greeted us from the desk facing the front of the elevator. She came toward us and graciously accepted Pat's overnight bag which contained two new pair of frivolous pastel baby-doll pajamas, foam-tread slippers, a hairbrush, comb, deodorant stick, and a coloring book with crayons. The new toothbrush and paste we had purchased from the first-floor hospital gift shop to save some small excitement for good measure (Pat loved shopping, for *any*thing.)

St. Joseph's chapel, three streets away, was our next stop. *One day at a time now.* We must remember.

Dr. Hagerty had told us it would be three months before we would know if surgery had been successful. And if not?

"Then, *hip* rotation is involved, which will require hip surgery." Please God, no!

The next day was our twentieth anniversary. Prayer would be our only celebration.

A team of three pediatricians engaged by Dr. Hagerty would examine Patty and consult with him regarding her general fitness for the involved surgery. During the hours of surgery Saturday morning I don't know what I did to keep occupied. Arthur of course was working. Gail had just gotten a job at the new and modern Howard Johnson Restaurant over past the Queen City Bridge. The aqua and orange apron and uniform required home laundering and starching each day. Perhaps that is how I got through the agonizing morning, fighting the urge to call 6th Floor Pediatrics.

The afternoon was a week long. The weather, sticky and hot. I hazily nibbled on something requiring no preparation.

Mother and Eleanor called. No, I hadn't heard anything yet.

Arthur called from the plant, trying not to *seem* anxious.

"No. We just have to wait I guess."

Saturday in Pediatrics being what it is, I was not called. I took the initiative early in the afternoon. "Yes, it's over. Your daughter is still in the Recovery Room but you may come in for this afternoon's visiting hours. She should be down by then."

When Gail got off duty at Howard Johnson's she and I visited the hospital together. Pat was in a bed next to the door in a four-bed ward. She was very still, her eyes closed, her dark hair tousled and damp from perspiration. I was glad that I had shortened her hair when I gave her a home permanent before camp.

For fear of waking her, Gail and I stayed our distance, silent and studying Pat's small figure lying there.

The red-haired nurse was again on duty. She had little to converse about. What was there to say? The operation, this first one, was over. Success? Not even the surgeon himself would know.

There was a pillow at the foot of the bed. Pat's left leg enclosed in the still damp, ghost-white cast rested rigidly on the pillow with only the top of her toes exposed. Her other leg would be free for awhile.

Gail moved closer to her sister. There was a narrow white pan close to Pat's chin, ready for nausea. Pat stirred. The pan slid. Gail reached over to catch it just as Pat opened her drooping eyelids to grope for the pan. She looked miserable, her face contorted. "Hi," she said to her sister. Gail responded in a whisper attempting to be gay. "It's all over. How are you, Pat?"

"Ohhhhh kayyy," Pat drawled sleepily.

"That's good, Pat," Gail said as she planted a soft kiss on the warm brow. Pat fell back to sleep. Before five minutes were up, she became nauseous again. It was I who held the pan next, hoping I could smile for her. Once at least.

I glanced over at the other three young patients. Girls. One with legs in traction. She couldn't have been more than five years old. The other two were about eight and eleven. They were nonchalant so we knew they could not have been admitted too recently or else nothing much was wrong with them.

"Hyyyyyy . . . ," a faltering voice was coaxing. It was Pat. Gail was stooping to pick up a crayon which had fallen to the floor for the little patient in traction.

"Hello, Pat," I kissed her. My knees felt weak. "How nice that it's done now."

"Yeahhh."

A large figure of a serious man crowded the doorway, shirt-sleeves buttoned at the cuff, tie in place, but no coat. No doctor jacket.

Without mistake it was our Dr. Hagerty.

"How are you, Girl?" spoken in the tone he saved for children. He was facing his patient, with his back to Gail and me.

Pat looked at him. He tried again. "How are you, Girl?"

One more glassy look. Then her lips parted with

extra effort. "Thanks," then a tired pause, "thanks for fixing—my—leg, dokturr."

His shirt moved with the deep breath he took. Gail and I looked in wonderment at each other. Pat wasn't fully out of the effects of anesthesia, yet she could not wait another minute to express her gratitude to the man who had maneuvered the scalpel!

Exhaling, and completely disarmed, Dr. Hagerty raised a large hand, patted the lifeless plaster-of-paris cast three times, and said, "That's okay, Chum!" With not so much as a backward glance for us, he sped out the door and down the hall. The man who seemed so tough, could not trust himself to hear more from the still-weak lips of the petite, brain-injured patient he had examined regularly from the time she was three years old and only vaguely able to sound out her own name.

We left to allow Pat more needed rest. Arthur would see her tonight. We stopped by Grandmother's to relieve her of her worries.

That evening Pat was shaking and weepy and needed constant embracing. Very infantile. We had not seen her like this since the earliest days of going to the therapy center. As we hovered nearby she would despairingly pull us closer and want to be hugged, first by her Daddy, then by me. Then by any nurse who happened by.

It was distressing to Arthur. Neither one of us knew what to make of it. We would just have to wait it out. It would be pointless to discuss it with the nurses. Cerebral palsied children come in such great varieties and our child we knew better than any strange nurse could possibly know in the course of only a few days.

We were wondering if they had had any difficulties getting her down to surgery in the first place. We learned later; before surgery two student nurses stood watch by her until sleep caught up with her. They wore surgical masks. We could hardly forgive ourselves. We had completely overlooked the fact of her terror of masks of any kind! Masks remain her one solitary fear, a phobia which defies analyzing. Any anxiety she felt regarding surgery we couldn't help, but we could have clued Dr. Hagerty in concerning the masks and Pat may then have been spared seeing these. We had not visualized Pat's being awake at all before she was lifted from her bed to be taken to the operating room.

Mother and Eleanor had their first visit with Pat the following afternoon and found her much the same —bordering on hysteria.

Pat's nerves seemed so shattered.

But we couldn't encourage so much weeping and hugging and kissing. *We* could afford it. But could *she*? This was only the first operation. There would be another one to come. And a third, maybe, involving twice the pain and misery.

We slowly began to move away from her side a little more each time we visited. We took turns visiting the other patients in the room, conversing with the parents. Gail took to brushing the little blond girl's hair, and helping her paste and cut for her scrapbook. Then she would return to Pat's bedside, manicuring her nails or dressing Pat's hair. Gail told Pat why Sheila was in traction; she had run suddenly between two parked cars and out in to the path of a heavy truck, intending to cross the street.

Pat listened without curiosity or interest.

It was a wonderful children's nurse who supplied the spoiling that now we couldn't indulge Pat in. The nurse's name was Miss Evelyn. She was close to forty and she was like a mother hen. Never too much in a hurry to listen to each young patient. They were her life. Even while she was at the other end of the ward re-doing a bed or straightening out a cluttered bedstand, she would hear every child's word directed at her.

Soon Pat stopped being so morose. When Miss Evelyn would come to Pat and put the foot pillow back in its proper place she would sing along in tune with Pat's portable radio, set always for Station WKBR.

"I think I'll turn it to FEA, Pat," she would tease, while reaching in the direction of the station knob.

Ordinarily, this would have bothered Pat, since WKBR was Gail's choice and whatever her sister did was the *only* smart thing to do. Gail was "IT" with Pat. Now, Miss Evelyn was to learn that she too was. "Okay. 'FEA if you want."

"Aw shucks, Pat, I thought you were going to give me an argument."

"No," Pat revealed affectionately, "I *like* you."

It was as simple as that, always, with Pat.

That evening Gail brought Raymond Ayotte with her, the boy she had been seeing on several dates. He took Gail to his senior prom at Bishop Bradley High School. They brought three sundaes from the nearest soda fountain. When we came in, the patient and her two seated visitors were "digging in" with plastic spoons, chattering away.

"When you get out of here, Pat," Gail was saying, "have Mom drive you and Grammy over to Howard Johnson's and I'll personally make you an ice-cream soda like you've never tasted before! You know how Grammy likes hers with not a whole lot of fizz? Well, you can tell me when to stop the fizz." Pat was laughing. That would be a novelty—her sister, a soda-jerker.

We told her what we had ourselves recently realized that the front passenger seat in the Rambler could be completely reclined so for the balance of the summer

174

while her left leg would be outstretched (ballpoint signatures were finally giving the cast a friendlier look), she could be taken to Howard Johnson's and other places perched in the far right of the back seat with her cast resting on the firm, lounge-like flat seat.

"Like Queen Elizabeth, Pat!" her father said. She took another dip into the melting vanilla ice cream and smiled enthusiastically.

Visiting hours ceased to climax with tears. Pat felt assured that each day meant two sessions with visitors. Her aunts and uncles and various family friends were dropping into the hospital now that the post-operative hysteria was past.

On the sixteenth day, Dr. Hagerty discharged Pat from the hospital. Arthur located the bracket for adjusting the car seat and we drove excitedly up to the emergency entrance. Two nurses were waiting beside Pat in her wheelchair, one of them holding the crutches and small overnight case, a philodendron plant and an empty vase in which flowers had arrived. A nun walked by and spoke a few parting words to Pat and wished us all luck.

We entered the house by our front door, close to where the open sofa bed was ready and waiting, with the new Kelly-green seven-way pillow, which was to serve so usefully during rides in the car as well as during convalescing hours on the lawn and in the living room.

Sister Mary Carmel with Sister Mary Benita of Gail's school visited during the following week, highlighting the whole convalescent period for Pat. Gail made cool drinks out in the kitchen and brought them in, remaining to chat. Sister Benita was telling her of the changes made for the coming school year. There would be a new principal, for example. Privileged information, this early in the summer.

175

When Gail departed with one of her girlfriends from the neighborhood, Sister Benita exclaimed, "Your daughter enjoys a very special esteem among her classmates, Mrs. StCyr. A lovely girl!"

"Thank you, Sister. She rates pretty high with her family too. We are twice blessed."

Chapter 16

*T*he four-foot wide hall that led to the bathroom gave Pat more than enough room for her crutches which she spread further apart than necessary. Sometimes, Gail insisted on carrying Pat from the bathroom to the sofa instead of bothering with the crutches. I disapproved. The long cast was heavier than Pat herself. Rather than have it become an issue, I relented. To myself, I would recall the tender picture which has become the symbol for Boystown, America: "He's not heavy, Father. He's my brother!" In Gail's case, it was a literal blood strain forming the bond between the two.

Pat's shampoos took a bit of ingenuity from both Gail and me. We would push the kitchen table up next to the counter which flanked the deep kitchen sink using the two hard, square cushions from the fireplace hearth to make a flat, even, five-foot rest to lay Pat on her back. From there I could proceed alone to shampoo her hair. The whole preparation would set us all to laughing. If she had money, we told Pat, the tip alone for this deluxe service would set her back plenty.

Gail began realizing on her own that lifting Pat was too strenuous and certainly not helping Pat. One morning while I was defrosting the neglected refrigerator, a furor was beginning in the living room.

"I can't!" yelped Pat.

"Of course you *can,* Pat," her sister was saying.

"I can't. I can't. I CAN'T; you hear me Gail?" Her voice was demanding, anger welling up in her.

"*Why* can't you?" Gail demanded.

"LEAVE me alone," Pat ordered.

Gail's own temper flared, "No, I won't leave you alone," she said crisply. "You have to get to the bathroom. I'm willing to help you. You just have to try, that's all." With that assertion, Gail went to start the right crutch forward to waste not another solitary minute.

I heard every word from the kitchen but I felt I shouldn't intrude. I'd noticed the irritability growing in Pat the last few days and it too much resembled that which filled the first days after surgery. My own nerves were on edge because of it.

Gail was determined.

Instinct warned me that something was about to happen.

The crutches in place, Pat was standing with all her weight leaning on the leg wearing the brace. She was refusing to advance with the rubber-soled orthopedic canvas boot, laced over her left foot in cast. I reached the archway just in time to see Pat raise her arm and strike Gail's face with an open palm.

I was as shocked as Gail. I motioned somehow to her not to react in kind. I would talk to her in a minute. She left for her bedroom. I knew she could

178

not half-imagine the involvements to Pat's nervous system. It takes more than merely living under the same roof. Arthur and I at our age were still learning.

Physically Pat's hand could not inflict a stinging blow for the same reason she could not engage in an easy game of softball; she lacked the force to drive a ball.

I returned Pat to a lying-down position atop the light sheets and let her cry the flood of tears that her sharpness with Gail had merely postponed.

I had only yesterday called Dr. Hagerty to see if he could explain the erratic behavior. Was there something obvious to him, that just wouldn't be to a mere layman? "No," he said. I supposed that he felt it was the result of coddling which parents are prone to do when kids are still in the process of recovery or something concerned with her being just cerebral-palsied.

"I can't walk, Ma," she was appealing to me, "I caannn't."

"Why can't you, Pat?" I asked, hiding my distress which would not be possible much *longer*. I was thinking, too, of my other daughter, needing explanations and an apology.

"It hurts, hurts, hurts," her voice rose.

"We can't understand why it should hurt now, Pat. You've been happy up to a few days ago. Now you strike Gail when she is being so nice to you."

She offered no explanation. She looked preoccupied, turning her head away from me.

Then, suddenly, she faced me again and asked, "Is my leg off, Ma?"

"Off? What do you mean, *off?*" I said impatiently.

"Like Uncle Paul?" she continued, her chin quivering as she rubbed her eyes.

"Oh my God! No"—Arthur's brother-in-law was, long before Pat was even born, operated on for one leg, only to lose it just above the knee. A few Sunday evenings Patty had seen him without his prosthesis when the stump was giving him discomfort.

"Why of course not, Pat. No, no, no. You can see your toes sticking out there at the bottom, can't you?" I said.

"Yesss," she said, still needing reassurance.

"Well, if your leg had been amputated, you wouldn't have your toes either."

She wasn't totally convinced, "But it *hurts.*"

"Well maybe that's from something else. We wouldn't lie to you, Pat. Have we ever lied to you?"

"No."

"Well, we're certainly not going to begin to now, either."

She was a little better as I straightened out her sheets, set her cast on the pillow at the foot of the sofa and went for a wet cloth to cool her face. The days were still very hot, and we had to keep two fans going in the house.

Pat's moods did not change. My stamina at a complete end, I called Dr. Hagerty to discuss it just once more, explaining in full detail. We were at wit's end. Nothing at all soothed Pat. She continued to say the walking hurt her. Doctor told me to hold the line until he returned with his file on Pat. (It had been forty-five days since surgery.)

"Well, she still has a couple or three weeks before the cast should be replaced by a shorter one." He stopped talking for a moment in order to concentrate, "But I guess we'll try taking it off tomorrow and get a look at things. Get her into the hospital first thing in the morning," he said.

When he removed the cast, he found the heel badly

blistered. Soon there would have been an infection. "That's from the cast touching the pillow at this point," he said in exasperation. That pillow was not supposed to ever be placed as far forward as the heel."

"We thought we were being careful of that; even the nurses had not always been able to keep it so."

"Well, this could have been prevented. Look at the discomfort this girl has suffered because of it."

The blister served as a graphic lesson, to all of us, for the next time.

After three days' rest in the hospital and now wearing a new cast to below the knee, Pat came home. It was August 26.

She sat upright in the *front* seat of the car, this time, and maneuvered like a pro, so relieved to bend the knee and leg.

*P*at's second operation would not be undertaken until early in the following spring due to the difficulties experienced from the first operation. On October 3 the short cast was removed and we had our first glimpse of the horizontal incision below the outer ankle. Only a faint trace of the blister was evident.

We had brought in her left shoe and brace as advised from the closet where it had been since July 6. To evaluate the results of the operation they would put both braces on and nurses and Doctor would observe the walking. She would still be dependent on crutches and lacking in confidence.

She did considerably well and would improve with home practice. "Get her a pair of straight-last high shoes," the doctor said. "I'll write out the prescription for you. Once you have them, they will need transferring to the braces."

Pat was released from the hospital in two days.

*G*ail's school was planning a Harvest Hop. With pumpkins ripened in the fields, Gail got me driving out to farms to get some along with cornstalks and borrowed bales of hay.

The few cornstalks that we found in over an hour's search the next day were limp this late in the month but Gail said, "So what? We're bringing the fields into the city. The girls all know that isn't easy."

She was so right. When the girls came running out of the school with their equally-spirited nun trailing close behind, their nervousness subsided. When they saw our half-opened trunk bearing pumpkins, hay and cornstalks, they showed great relief. Back there in the gym, their crepe paper streamers and matching motifs were finished more than an hour ago. They wanted that dance to be a whopping success and they had very little time left what with their homework yet to do. The only thing we hadn't brought them was the pitchfork. But the aroma was sufficient.

One shapely miss held her nose! "Barns are like that," Gail chided. "You don't find hay in cedar-lined closets, you know."

After I picked Pat up from Grandmother's I hastily sprayed the rear floor and trunk of the car with Fuller's Lavendar Scent. Since that day, Arthur never again allowed me to spray it *any*where.

The school Caedmon Club which was responsible

for this dance wasn't Gail's only extracurricular activity. She was Class Treasurer, a member of the choral group, and on the Student Council.

When she was chosen for one of the leads in the senior play to be held later on in the year and a singing/dancing part in the musicale "Those Wonderful Years," we never stopped wondering how she would fit it all in.

There would be much more than this too, the closer they came to graduation day. It made a busier year for me as well. When the day before Christmas, a huge van backed into the driveway and two men carried in a limed-oak hope chest with Gail's name on the delivery order, Arthur and I experienced a strong wave of despair. Gail, only seventeen, was being too forcefully *rushed*. But aside from not wishing to mar the most beautiful of holidays, we did not trust ourselves to speak right then. We decided to wait for just the right moment.

From a hidden nook in our basement, I brought up the complete tea set of delicate china once owned by Gail's great-grandmother long departed. It was blue and gold with a floral pattern. Then I dug out a brand new pair of slender crystal salt and pepper shakers (things which Gail hadn't seen up until then).

These I gave her for the new hope chest; it looked so empty and every time we passed it, it kept reflecting our own feelings. As she was admiring my contribution, I suggested calmly that it was not marriage itself that we were opposed to for this in our eyes was a woman's greatest fulfillment.

"I know," she looked earnestly back at me, trying to fathom a parent's reasoning; gifts like these gladdened any girl's heart. Why did her parents appear so grave over this one? We did not wish Gail to have a hard life, or serious problems too soon.

*P*at had dismissed her crutches and was walking well on her own. It was a free stride, without halt. So good to see!

When New Year's Eve came Arthur and I let our hair down at the Deerhead Sportsman's Club of which Arthur was a member.

Within less than two months, Gail broke briefly with Raymond, telling us, "I can't seem to think." Well, there's no need to rush, Gail. We *all* need thinking time.

During this spell, she went tobogganing and walking with her cousin Lou. She was with him a great deal. It took the place of dating. It was months later before we learned that Gail's quandry had been over an engagement ring Raymond had purchased and was urging her to take.

Now it was March. The pussy willows had just begun to bud out in the marsh beyond our kitchen casements. Soon it would be time to bring Pat into Sacred Heart Hospital for her second operation.

Raymond returned to the family picture. No diamond had been accepted.

*O*n March 29 sedation proved far more effective in getting Pat into surgery without the same degree of alarm she had suffered for the first leg. Too, she knew what to expect.

There was not the same infantile behavior this time. She had been familiarly greeted by her good friend, Miss Evelyn; this too had been very comforting to her.

Pat's stay this time involved only nine days as compared to sixteen for the left leg. The turn necessary to the right foot was not as extreme, therefore there was less pain following surgery.

The cast would be shortened in mid-May. Spring would be in full bloom. How very much this can mean to a bogged-down New Englander!

Behind closed doors, Gail had been studying her lines for the play, as well as the mannerisms and gait. It wasn't at all easy. Her role was that of Solly Levine, male promoter to a promising boxer whose sister was a postulant in the holy order. The name of the play was "Dowry for Moira." The script called for a rabbit's foot or some such luckpiece in the hip pocket plus an east-side big city lingo.

To complete her costume, Gail had dug up an old pair of her father's fishing sneakers, a pair of faded trousers from a classmate's brother, her own coarse knit, khaki turtleneck sweater and a visor cap. Any resemblance between Solly Levine and the magnetically pretty miss so recently gowned in ruffled peau de soie was purely coincidental.

Until that afternoon of the play, she had not allowed us to see her in the masculine get-up. Her hair was pasted severely under the cap as Solly followed his not-so-confident prodigy into the hushed convent to solicit the efficacious prayer of Sister Moira whose dowry her brother's prize money was apparently destined for. Prayer, *plus* a rabbit's foot, thought Solly, would make the title a cinch!

Each time Solly strode across the stage in bursting enthusiasm for the upcoming bout we had to remind ourselves that this was our Gail! Her paternal grandfather, Harry T. StCyr, was undoubtedly applauding from his grave, having been in his earlier years a travelling acrobatic comedian accompanied by Arthur's sister Mabel. When vaudeville days gave way to talking movies, he still hadn't been able to resist the environment of the theater; from then until his death he ran the movie reels at Manchester's leading cinema.

Youthful applause broke out as the small cast from "Dowry for Moira" took their bows. Before Gail reached home Pat and I had a party table set for supper with fresh cut flowers for the ingenue from Ferretti's Market. Arthur had a congratulatory card hidden in his pocket with a crisp bill for a surprise. Departing for her date that night, Gail was in lighter spirit. The exhausting rehearsals were over. All had gone well. Only the Jazz-Age dance routine of the "Twenties" was left to perfect for the musicale "Wonderful Years."

May 9, seniors met at the Knights of Columbus Hall for their "Tea" sponsored by St. Joseph High Juniors.

May 14, Pat's cast was shortened at the hospital.

May 27, the Mother-Daughter Tea, delightfully served, was held in the school's auditorium.

Gail attended her senior prom with Raymond on June 1.

Two weeks later, she was graduated with her sixty-six classmates.

While she turned in her rented graduation robe and cap, a dozen long-stemmed American Beauty roses waited backstage from her grandmother and Aunt Eleanor. We had presented her with a platinum wristwatch. She had received other gifts and she had them proudly displayed atop her hope chest beside the bouquet Raymond had delivered.

Arthur's family and mine congregated outside the school for a leisurely few minutes, then sped for home to begin filling the dishes and percolating the coffee for twenty-two guests. The relatives began to arrive gayly, with Gail, Raymond and young Lou somewhere among them. Every door and window was opened for a maximum of air. Everyone was talking at once and lightly joking while we invited them to start helping themselves. We continued our party while Gail and Raymond were excused to join the other new graduates and their escorts in town.

On July 3, by the time Pat had her short cast removed and new straight-last high shoes transferred to her braces (she would continue with braces for another short while) Gail was settled into her new job in the Accounting Department of the New England Telephone Company.

Within the month Pat's feet looked so much better. It was almost certain that surgery had been 100% successful! No hip surgery would be necessary.

One rainy night, late in August, Gail returned home from her date with the diamond on her finger.

On January 5, she and Raymond were married.

Chapter 17

*T*hat summer, the thrill of seeing my first newspaper articles published helped all of us. The early weeks without Gail had not been easy. I'd go down into the basement to start the laundry and when I'd come back upstairs I would find Pat again sitting on a kitchen chair beside the telephone waiting for a call from Gail. I attempted talks with Pat, explaining that Gail was busy at her job plus keeping their apartment. It never helped.

So I allowed her to leave her chair by the phone until Arthur would return from work. Then it was needed out in the kitchen. The following morning would always find it back near the phone. Somehow we got through it.

While Mother kept Pat, I would drive the distances to interview the interesting couples whose stories I was working on. Then came September when the social functions crowded the page where my features had appeared. I needed the chance to fall-clean anyhow. Pat wasn't so sure she didn't prefer her mother carrying a pad, pencil and flash camera. She liked the new and contrasting gayety of it all.

But this autumn I would sew. I was putting on a few pounds. It was either the new compulsion to eat with losing Gail, figuratively of course, or the "O'Donnell Spread" as I nicknamed it when Eleanor began putting hers on. (My mother's family were always small until they hit their forties.)

Then I recalled those Cooks of the Week I had interviewed for the Manchester Union-Leader: they had had me sampling disastrously rich desserts. I added to the problem with the bonus-recipes I had smuggled while I was at it. No wonder my dresses were fraying at the seams. I would have to sew myself some of those new shift-dresses. When Christmas and New Year's Eve came around, my waistline was concealed.

I decided to visit the young publisher of a nearby weekly newspaper, only a few streets down from the Union-Leader office. Year-round they printed features similar to the kind I had just spent a summer on.

Donald Madden gave me the go-ahead and I wrote a page on HOW MANCHESTER LIVES, the story of a family of seven. I followed it with a profile on the chief librarian in the Children's Room of the City Library, a Miss Arlene Thorp. So much for the added weight and creative-writing attempts.

Now it was Friday, November 22.

Every Friday I went into town to shop and attend to any business at the paper. Today I would pick up family cards for Thanksgiving, only six days away.

Since I now had less perseverance than formerly, I conducted my most urgent business first, should weariness overtake me. Then I would return to where the Rambler was parked and go straight home. Seldom did Pat have Friday supper with us; it was the unwritten promise between Grandmother and her. Being

190

alone gave me the hour to file away receipts and papers on any business transacted during that day to make a record for the following Friday and to clear my mind.

In all my rushing, I failed to notice the faces of downtown shoppers. This was not rare of course, since many of our friends have said they passed me on the street, tried to hail me, but I looked lost in my thoughts. I was. Particularly then. When my hands weren't busy, my mind was.

As I thumbed through the various Thanksgiving cards in the stationery store a small portable radio was playing. I was looking for HUSBAND cards. How easy is it to find a new one after twenty-two years? Especially for a loving husband like Arthur, so unselfish, always finding new amazing ways to comfort me when I grew darkly discouraged. Sometimes it was silence he offered. Sometimes the order to buy myself some new costume jewelry, something not easily afforded in times past. Or a drive with me to some new place we hadn't tried for a gourmet special. With each passing year I could only appreciate him more.

"They're bringing in the coffin now. Every one here looks grossly numb, and *frozen* . . . cradled in . . . wife's arms . . . rushed from blood-spattered limousine . . . Connally hit . . . in head and wrist . . ."

I couldn't concentrate. Why do stores tune on radios? Ceiling music is fine, and even soothing, but news broadcasts?

The cashier looked drained. I looked to the left of me. No one ELSE was buying any cards. Not even searching. A businessman was saying something solemn to the male proprietor of the shop. Whatever was *wrong?* What happened, to affect these strangers so?

The radio played on. ". . . assassin's bullets . . . open car."

"Has something happened in Manchester?" I asked.

191

"The President has been *shot*." She spoke in a whisper.

"The President!" I said, ashamed that I hadn't listened more carefully to the broadcast still going on. "Is he hurt badly?" I asked. "He is dead," she reported gravely.

My mouth fell open. I took a step ahead then stopped. Had I heard right? This was only a nightmare. Or was something happening to my equilibrium. It could. The years with Pat, the two operations, Gail's teenage marriage. Newlyweds so young—such a worry these days. Not to mention my temporary jobs. The writing. Was keeping so busy good for me or was I pushing my luck? My blood pressure, only recently high, required pills. They were running low. I was due for another check-up.

"President KENNEDY?" I said.

"Yes," she replied with finality.

I wanted to get out of the store fast. I no longer wanted the cards I had so carefully chosen. But I felt awkward about putting them back. That too would require concentration. I numbly paid for them and walked out onto a street almost deserted except for some high-schoolers heading in the opposite direction from me. I looked at them. Three of the girls had tear-stained faces. It was true then. It was a nightmare, a living one.

The cards seemed such a frivolous purchase. Our young President had just been assassinated and I was sentimentally pondering over greeting cards. No wonder people have left the streets! No wonder the teenagers were moved to tears. This generation of non-thinkers? No, not on your life! This President had promised them so much. For them, too, the world had stopped this very afternoon.

When I reached home, I threw off my high-heeled pumps. My feet were tired. The phone rang.

"Hello," I said.

"Peggy, it's Mom. You'd better come get Pat. She looks very ill."

"The President's dead, Mom," I said, still unable to grasp the meaning of the words.

"Yes. We were watching television when they broke in with that terrible news. This is what is wrong with Pat. She's very white and looks spent." Mom was not one to dramatize. "I've been ringing you for quite a while hoping you'd have heard it."

I went right down. Even if I had learned of the assassination as early as most had, I would never have given a thought to Pat's concern for it. We knew she enjoyed all of JFK's video speeches. In fact, she would sit completely through them. No matter what Arthur or I would have been doing at the time, Pat would insist that we join her to hear him.

Pat was inconsolable. I took her home without saying too much.

Over the last two years, Pat had matured and somehow I couldn't treat her much differently than I would Gail during personal moments.

"Let's lie down awhile, Pat; I'm tired too."

We stretched ourselves across the chenille-draped double bed which is Arthur's and mine. We didn't sleep. We just held hands.

*I*t was the start of a new year. Nineteen hundred and sixty-five.

Except for the daytime soap operas which she had become addicted to, Pat had nothing to do. The prospect of her future grieved both Arthur and me. It was worse for me, I believe, because I was faced with it every waking hour of every day and couldn't forget it.

I am not a television fan especially, and particularly not in the daytime. But it filled Pat's empty world. Such idleness for her depressed me more with each passing day. In such a state of mind, I found myself conversing less and less with her. She, realizing this change, tried not to intrude upon my preoccupation. I had lost all of my old resilience.

It was on one day when I was able to bring my thoughts back to home and the present that I hit upon the idea to teach Pat to DANCE. Yes, to dance. For no practical reason. When would she ever use the dancing? But it would give her something to try for. It might lift me out of this uncomfortable mental-dullness, too.

"Would you like to learn to dance, Pat?" I asked, mustering a semblance of cheer. She didn't take her eyes off the video screen, but I knew that she had heard me.

"No," she answered politely but without interest.

"Yes, Pat, I think it might turn out to be fun."

She made no comment. But I felt I had hit upon a good idea. Her feet were beautifully straight now. She had been in low shoes without braces for over one year.

But after she stood and I took her waist and tried slowly to lead her to the organ music played by Ken Griffin on a Columbia long-playing record, I found her as stiff and hard to move as a two hundred pound cigar-store Indian! As a dancing partner and not the leader she would have to walk in reverse rather than forward. This made her every bit as apprehensive as when she had been a child practicing to leave the wall for that first time.

All the music was in three-quarter time, soft and melodic. With her reluctance to back up, I grasped her belt tighter so that she could better feel the support I was giving her.

"I won't let you go, Pat," I promised as I progressed from one foot to the other, pushing the fronts of her shoes until she would be less rigid and possibly stimulated with the reminiscent rhythm.

We made no turns, just moved in a straight line, then walked back to the point of beginning and repeated the route.

Pat felt no enthusiasm. But then this was nothing new for the last several months. As each romantic waltz began to play I would reflect on this inevitable time in the life of a retardate; after society and the family have brought the child this far, where does he go from here? A life of cloister and boredom. By this time Mother and Dad have reached middle age. For the retardate, "Sorry, this is the end of the line," in the teens, when life in a sense is just beginning for most. My anger grew.

We started again with "Our Heartbreaking Waltz"; it was the best because it was slightly slower than the others. How applicable the title! Then to "Roses." The "Cecile Waltz" was just fast enough to increase Pat's rigidity so I took to picking up the needle and placing it on only those slower numbers which helped us in our new venture.

At the end of each session in the mornings to follow my arm ached from the tight grip on Pat's waist. She was beginning to relax and move the feet more easily. As she did, I could release my hold a little more each day.

"La dee dah, la dee dah, la dee dum," I found myself

195

singing soon. Not too long afterward, Pat as well seemed to be enjoying her achievement and became more spontaneous to it. I was able to help her develop the light, swaying movement in her torso which every waltzer must eventually learn. Pat would never succeed at it completely.

We advanced to making half and three-quarter turns. It had taken three weeks before she could say that she knew how to dance. When we showed her Dad, his eyes filled. He commented on the added confidence the dancing had promoted.

Once the dancing was mastered, we slipped back to the dull pattern immediately preceding its idea. I had a growing fear that this was the way it was going to be from here on in. I had grown incurably tired now. Even my mind did not wish to function the way it used to.

Pat's own recently developing silence also disturbed me. Where would her companionship be for the years ahead. Wasn't there some place where she could be trained with other girls just like herself? A place to live, perhaps, and enjoy a dignity learning domestic tasks, the daily accomplishment experienced by nearly every other young woman? I knew the time had come for me to talk this all over with Arthur.

The next Friday evening, after we had eaten leisurely (Pat's day with Grandmother and Eleanor), I began describing the change in Pat to Arthur, how afraid I was of what was happening to myself, and what did he think of our looking for a residential home for our daughter?

Arthur paled. Then, "No, not that, Peg," he answered softly. "Why can't we have a woman come in to be a companion for Pat and at the same time give you a hand where necessary?"

"Arthur, I've thought of that too. How easy would

it be to find a steady kind woman who would want this type of job?"

"Peg, I'll find an extra job, anything, to help you keep Pat at home."

"But that won't be best for Pat, Arthur. And I don't want anything to happen to you, for heaven's sake! I know I'm slipping fast. It frightens me. I've thought more about this than I can afford to now." He said he understood my fatigue.

I asked him to please give the whole matter very serious thought. I knew I needn't have. He would think of little else until he reached some conclusion. When he brought Pat back from my Mother's that evening, she was carrying with her some knitting which Eleanor had attempted to teach her. It surprised us that Pat could learn such a thing. Now, wouldn't it be nice if . . .

The next morning I decided to call other mothers of girls of Pat's age to see how they were occupying their days and evenings. One mother had taken her daughter to the Manchester Therapy Center from the time she was two years old. Her sixteen year old was enrolled in programs for the adult handicapped that were held sporadically. During those weeks when they were non-existent the girl would languish around the house. "Sometimes she doesn't even care to comb her hair. She leaves her bed unmade and I can't seem to cheer her up at all."

She went on, "But during the periods when the program is in full swing at the Community Center, she's an altogether different person. She virtually flies around the house in the morning, making her bed, grooming herself, and catching the bus to be there early!" Her daughter was a mild spastic with fewer limitations than Pat.

I called another mother. Her son was a nineteen-year-old cerebral palsied. "Oh, he's not doing much at all," she told me. "But his energy far outweighs ours. We retire at night at eleven o'clock. We laughingly say he puts us to bed! He watches TV long after we're asleep. He lets the cat out and in, bolts the door and likes to be the last one to go to bed." He was a more severely involved case of cerebral-palsy than Pat.

The mother had told me that when she had nearly reached a nervous breakdown not too long before, her husband had appealed to an influential politician to help get her son into the State Institution for the Mentally Retarded. So far it had not succeeded. They were still waiting. On and on it went, the story unchanged. The one Sheltered Workshop in Manchester proper had a very limited registration; shortage of teachers as well as funds.

We vaguely remembered reading about a residential home sometime back in the weekly Free Press. I visited the periodical-room of the City Library to search for the page which featured it. I found it in one of the August issues of two years back. The article said that it was a rehabilitation center and accredited school for 22 emotionally disturbed, physically handicapped and mentally retarded patients. It was located an hour and thirty minutes from our home just before the Vermont Line. It was owned by two women, one a retired Army nurse, the other a registered occupational therapist whose experience had been in mental hospitals and in homes for defective children. We made the trip there on the following Sunday when, once again, Pat stayed with her Grandmother.

Cedarcrest, as the home was called, sat on the very top of a steep driveway. The home was huge, with ells and additions everywhere, put on as the registration grew (the home had begun with only three children). The interior was charming and ever so color-ful.

Only the former nurse was in that afternoon and it was she who showed us the various departments and functions of each. Here, as at Kennedy Foundation in Brighton, Massachusetts, they also had a few hopeless ones. Crib cases. It is hard to look at these.

There was a spacious gym down in the basement. Small tricycles were speeding across the concrete floor ridden by one obviously-retarded little boy and two seemingly more normal boys. Colorful education toys were strewn about on the gay linoleum floor.

We described Pat, her limitations, and her age.

"Of course you probably realize that homes like these already have a waiting list?"

"Well, soon it will be urgent for us to find a suit-able answer for Pat."

"Yes, of course, her age is against her. Most of our children come here at a much earlier age. Even our oldest girl is younger than your Patricia."

"May we ask what the tuition here is?"

She quoted a $200-per month figure!

"I could go to work while she's away," I said.

"It still poses a burden for any couple. Other ex-penses unexpectedly come up. For some of the cases public agencies handle the cost. There are many state wards and foster children in need of places like ours, you know. You are welcome to visit here anytime. I can't say when there would be an opening. Of course, for everyone's benefit, we would have to have the case history on your daughter should we decide to make any exception concerning her age."

We left there feeling we had at least begun to in-sure Pat's future.

Soon I told Pat, not sure of what her reaction might be. "We're looking for a school, Pat, where you will have other girls to talk to and do things with every day."

Enthusiastically she asked, "Where? When?"

"We don't know yet. We're asking other parents and we have visited two places, but they weren't especially for girls your age. Mostly younger children."

"Oh," she said, agreeing that younger children wouldn't do.

Only after several days of investigation did I learn that no places such as we had in mind existed in the State of New Hampshire, short of the state institution for the mentally retarded.

Did they train teenage retardates in workshops?

"Some," the last parent told me, "but very few. It's a place for them to stay, be fed, sleep, and be supervised. They do train them as much as they can in self-care. The attendants who work there are truly dedicated."

With each passing day the matter became more pressing. We had nothing to lose by looking into the state school. One paid for such care only according to one's means. The child was able to visit home periodically and on holidays provided the child was not impossible to handle on his return to the school.

Chapter 18

On February 3, I visited the school and was taken on a leisurely tour of the grounds and some of the buildings by the school's superintendent, Mr. Arthur E. Toll. He was very honest about what they did *not* have at the school, but he was equally hopeful about the future and proud of the progress that had been made. The Laconia State School was begun in the year 1900 and the early buildings all had three floors. Each floor housed from thirty to forty-five children. In the whole institution there were just under one thousand patients. It did not have what anyone would call a resemblance to home. But Mr. Toll said they were improving conditions as rapidly as the Legislature would appropriate funds for it. "Most appropriations are devoted to public highways as you know, and not enough for all the things we'd like to do here."

As he took me through the overcrowded workshop —boys at manual training, girls at a few outmoded sewing machines—he said that additional shops were greatly needed if the school were to help a sufficient number of those with the capacity to learn such skills.

Then he took me through the one new, ultra-modern low and rambling brick home-like affair which housed girls of Pat's age. I was thrilled at the sight of it, "How many more of such type buildings will there be?"

"We have been promised none," he answered.

The "Cottage Program" was designed for those who had the potential for returning to society and becoming self-supporting. The cottage was staffed by a cottage "father and mother" who lived in a compact apartment at the end of the building. It had lovely cozy bedrooms with blond furniture with two or three girls to each room. The dining area featured a large picture window overlooking the mountains of the Lakes Region.

The girls were taught proper social behavior, skills, grooming and how to handle money.

There were between fourteen and twenty girls at this time being prepared for the competition they would face in the outside world. Pat would not qualify for this cottage. Girls here had to be strong and capable enough to wash floors and do many other chores including tending children.

On March 24, we took Pat to Laconia for her evaluation. The usual records were requested. Not realizing the full implication of institutions, Pat was not as apprehensive as we.

A new building had gone up and was almost ready for occupancy when Pat was accepted. The new King Nursery would be housing 80 of the 5- to 10-year-old boys and girls. This would relieve other buildings and with some careful juggling, older applicants on the waiting list could now be accepted into the various older buildings. The letter of admission arrived. The date: May 4, 2:00 P.M.

Pat's excitement grew as she saw me bring home new clothes, label them and pack them into her luggage. We bought her a new transistor radio and had her name lettered on the back. Gail asked Pat if she'd like some nylon stockings (her first pair) to take to the new school. "No Gail," said Pat, "I wouldn't look nice in nylons."

She was one day to change her mind.

***

*T*he day came for Pat to be admitted to the State School. We would not be allowed to visit her for thirty days. The plaque which Rose had given us a few days before was propped strategically over our stove where it would do the most good. It was Reinold Neibuhr's "God grant me the serenity to accept the things I cannot change; courage to change the things I can; and wisdom to know the difference." We were not feeling our anticipated loss alone. We had relatives, all warm and genuine.

The weather was beautiful. Pat herself was relatively anxious. She was looking forward to meeting a new group of girls her own age. She again gave us courage, this child of love.

Once inside the building where our daughter would reside, we were aghast at the varying ages of the girls. On the sun-porch were women in their forties, a few without teeth. Their figures were matronly.

Pat was numbed by what she saw. It would only be speculation on our parts to say what exactly she was feeling. The attendants, none of them, made any comment. Looking back, I know now that their experience had taught them the seriousness of impact of Admission Day for both parents and child. In their neat white uniforms and attractively coiffured hair, they left nothing to be desired. We scanned the long row of forty beds in the immaculate dormitory. Home was such a contrast. None of the girls seemed to be *doing* anything. Just sitting!

They curiously studied Pat. I thought how strange it was that we never think of retarded children as ever growing pudgy, toothless, decrepit when, in fact, they're exactly like the rest of the human race. Here one could not escape the shocking reality.

Just before leaving, the attendant said gently, "Mail can be sent to Patricia. We encourage it. If she can't read sufficiently, it will be read to her."

The matter of mail was the last thought in our heads.

The lakes, the mountains, the hillsides all looked exactly as they had before we delivered Pat. The birds still sang. Nothing had changed. Except for us.

In three weeks a letter arrived written in a stranger's handwriting:

Dear Mother and Father:
I hope to see you very soon. I received twenty-one birthday cards yesterday (her first birthday away from home and family) also your letter today. Will you please thank all my relatives and friends for my lovely cards? I think of you and Dad always. I go outside every day and go to church on Sunday. I like it here and the kids are nice to me. It is pretty up here with the flowers that are around us.

I hope to see you both very soon.
With love,
Pat

On Decoration Day we were allowed to take her home for the three-day weekend. We found her dejected. Gail accompanied us. It was an emotional reunion with Pat for all of us. She hardly talked at all. We spoke of the waiting cake, candles, and belated gifts.

On Saturday we threw some summer clothes into a valise and spent the rest of the holiday at Eleanor's camp with Grandmother. Gail and Raymond came up on Sunday. Pat referred to Laconia State School, confidentially, to her Aunt Eleanor as "that place." She did not say it to Arthur and me. She refused to touch any food. She vomited anything that we urged her to consume. She was extremely unhappy. Only her cousins out in the water interested her. Thank God, there were a good number of them there. The school was not what she had expected it would be.

When we returned her, the compassionate supervisor reported how difficult the month had been for Pat. "She tried to bear up but one day she just fell apart in my arms, weeping inconsolably, telling me how she missed all of you."

In June when she came home she spent most of her day lying on the bed. I attempted to discourage it. That's what brought tears from her, tears that she had been trying not to cry.

"Ma, did you see the bathroom *up there?*"

"Not really, Pat."

"Everybody's in there at the same time," she charged.

"Can't be, Pat," I argued, "that room wouldn't hold very many."

"There's no door between us," she revealed, describing her humiliation very plainly.

I stood with my back to her because her breaking voice was sapping me of my courage. I began rearranging the clothes in her closet. She was beginning to talk and I felt she needed to very much. "The bed is low. LOW," she repeated, raising her voice. "Not like this one," she explained, touching the edge of her mattress. I must have sounded very unsympathetic when I answered, "Well, you won't have so far to fall from if you move too close to the edge, will you?" I looked squarely at her, having managed a smile of sorts. Her brown eyes flashed, angry, and impatient with me, the same way they had flashed when Gail wanted to force her to walk on crutches. That stopped all conversation.

She described the same things to her father.

"Well, that's the way it is for boys and girls going into the service, too, Pat," Arthur answered. "Army bunks, all in a row, and eating in Mess Halls."

Were we doing the right thing?

I went out of doors and worked peat moss into the soil of the rock garden Arthur had constructed out of the bank which separated the driveway from our back lawn and for which he had purposely built up the pleasing collection of rocks. Together we had consulted evenings over their placement the way we had with the multi-colored flagstone which made up our front walk.

It helped—digging the holes and preparing them for the new perennials which would provide a blaze of color throughout the summer and early fall. Showy petunias waited in boxes of a dozen in the self-service flowerland up the road. It helped.

*I*t was to take a year before our daughter's full adjustment was complete. Sometime during this period we were told of something which had happened to make the attendants realize that Pat StCyr was making it at last.

A new girl had been admitted and for the first day or two, like all the others, she sat melancholy and mute, shocked at the sudden separation from her family. Pat tried to talk to her. But she got no response. Then Pat came to a decision. She walked close to the newly-admitted girl and said, "You feel sad. You miss your folks, don't you?" The girl just stared back at Pat. But Pat had decided that she would not let that bother her.

"Well, I felt like that too when I first came here. I missed my folks. I cried. I didn't like it here." There was no break in Pat's stream of words. "But I got used to it." Only then did she allow herself a few seconds' recess. "You'll get used to it too."

The new little girl perked up. As of that very moment, she began to smile and talk and followed Pat the rest of the day. She was her sidekick going down to the dining room. Pat watched over her like a mother hen, from then on.

*P*atty and I were not long out of the road leaving the State School when she unexpectedly burst into laughter. It startled me.

207

"What are you laughing at, Pat?" I asked. It had been the very first time I'd been treated to her laughter since she had entered the school.

"Well, the other night something funny happened!"

"Oh yeah? What?" I said.

Well, we were all in bed for the night. Everything was nice and quiet—"

"And?" I prompted.

"I felt myself going to the floor. Then a loud noise and the kids all yelling for the 'tendants: "COME, COME, STCYR'S BED JUST BROKE!"

Thank you, God. Thank you for Pat's adjustment and restored humor.

*P*at had been staying at the school exactly fourteen months. Gail and Raymond had been married three and one half years. July 7th was to be our 25th Wedding Anniversary. In only two days, a hundred guests would be gathering at the nearby Massabesic Lake Beach House to help us celebrate this milestone in our lives.

We were solvent at last.

Eleanor was vacationing with us, along with Pat. (We were still mourning the loss of my Mother who had died suddenly September last. We had been successful in preparing Pat for such an inevitability.)

For the festivities there had been secret planning; Pat on the phone whispering things into the receiver to her sister. Gail and Raymond arrived with a cake and a gift—a sterling silver cake server inscribed at the local jewelers from them and Pat.

On Saturday morning Eleanor took Pat downtown

for a new teased hairdo. Pat would be wearing a sheer blush-pink short gown for which her sister and brother-in-law had dyed her oxford shoes to match. A popular orchestra had been engaged and Eleanor had readied the crystal punch bowl for its diced fruit and sparkling ingredients.

Pat was radiant and bright-eyed as she started to the car to depart for the Beach House.

"You look gorgeous, Pat. Gorgeous!" her father exclaimed.

She sighed and reddened, flustered by the compliment.

"Cut it out, Dad," she said.

It was Daune Chicoine, now seventeen and a tall exquisite beauty reuniting with her childhood friend after her family's six-year stay in Arizona, who was to exclaim: "Somehow, I never expected to find Pat so sophisticated."

At times we had to admit that Pat seemed just that. Sophisticated. Then if too strongly flattered or questioned, she could react as a little child. We had witnessed it so many times.

Arthur exchanged an amused glance with Eleanor as she settled into the seat beside her niece. Arthur walked back into the house, looked at the clock and said we had exactly forty-five minutes in which to dress for our big event.

He got into his summer-weight charcoal gray suit while I pulled out my lime-green chiffon cocktail dress.

Cymbidium orchids waited in the refrigerator from my darling beside his boutonniere.

While I was dressing, I heard the Pitmans come in, Tom and his wife, who were escorting us. The clink of glasses soon followed and when I entered the kitchen, Arthur was just opening the bottle of imported champagne he had been chilling. Growing a trifle nervous, we left the drinks unfinished as we realized that time was moving fast.

Eleanor, lovely in a brighter-than-usual two piece ensemble, was presiding over the punch bowl as we arrived, with Stella and Louise Merrill serving the more timid guests who remained seated in the lounge. Gail and Pat were at another corner conversing with women guests. Sylvia was just focusing her camera on them—Gail in her white lace over yellow, a head taller than her sister. (This was the occasion for which Pat agreed to wear her very first nylons.)

We were led to our places at the head table, where to Arthur's left stood the Right Reverend Monsignor John Foley, smiling and witty as always. He apologized ahead to Gail for the fact that he would have to leave his dinner almost untouched due to his stringent diet.

Mabel and Paul were seated to Pat's right. Tom offered a toast immediately following the hearty opening by Arthur's oldest friend from bachelor days, Dick Durette. Monsignor Foley said grace before the chicken would grow cold before us.

After dinner Pat was swept from one male to another, thrilled to her toes at her first experience at social dancing! Like a girl at her first prom. Her father first, then her brother-in-law, then uncles and young friends of Gail's and Raymond's.

It was a struggle to contain our happiness. The miraculous ease with which Pat danced such a long part of the evening! Tonight, she had danced upon a cushion of fleecy cloud. Tonight, she had felt a responsibility for this party for us, her parents. She couldn't have been more gratified.

When she finally arrived at the house after us on the arms of Gail and our son-in-law, she was wearing his ample size 38 suitcoat which reached almost to her knees. The sleeves were folded back at the wrist three times, exposing the lining. The evening had turned chilly. She could be overheard sublimely recalling her popularity of the last hours. She bubbled over with joy, laughed excitedly. Infectiously, Gail and Raymond laughed with her. Pat's telltale corsage, crushed from the evening's dancing, hung limp at her proud and erect shoulders. She couldn't wait to tell the girls at Laconia!

While we didn't voice all the things we were thinking, I know Arthur was reflecting as thoughtfully as I was, taking inventory of our lives.

Looking at his wonderful face I recalled the words on the very first card he ever sent me; against a rustic background, the words "Hinges of Friendship" were etched beside two long gold foil hinges. The inside message read:

May the
hinges of friendship
never
grow rusty.
HAPPY BIRTHDAY

and it was signed with a flourish.

The mere signature had turned my heart over.

Now, after all these busy years together, I had a question to ask.

Had they ever had the chance to?